Dover Harbour *Royal Gateway*



Published for the Dover Harbour Board
by Riverdale Publications
24 Riverdale
River
Dover CT17 0QX

*Designed by* www.whitegatedesign.co.uk

*Printed by* Buckland Press Ltd

ISBN 0-9536166-5-7

Henry VIII embarking
from Clark's Pier at Dover for
Field of Cloth of Gold, 1520

Dover Harbour

# Royal Gateway

*Celebrating 400 years of the*
*Dover Harbour Board 1606-2006*

*by* Derek Leach

# Contents

Eastern Docks, 2005

# Foreword

When considering how to celebrate the 400th anniversary of the granting of the Royal Charter to the Port of Dover by King James I in 1606, we decided not only to arrange suitable events to mark the occasion but also to sponsor a commemorative book about the harbour.

"Dover Harbour - Royal Gateway" is two books in one. It is a unique compilation of the port's association with royalty since 1606 as well as the history of the development of the port to the impressive successful international commercial operation that it is today.

Derek Leach combines knowledge of both the town and Port of Dover. Previously a senior manager of HM Customs & Excise at the port and currently the Chairman of the Dover Society, he has written this splendid book which so appropriately marks our 400th anniversary. On behalf of all who read this book, thank you Derek.

**R.K.Dibble**
Chairman
Dover Harbour Board

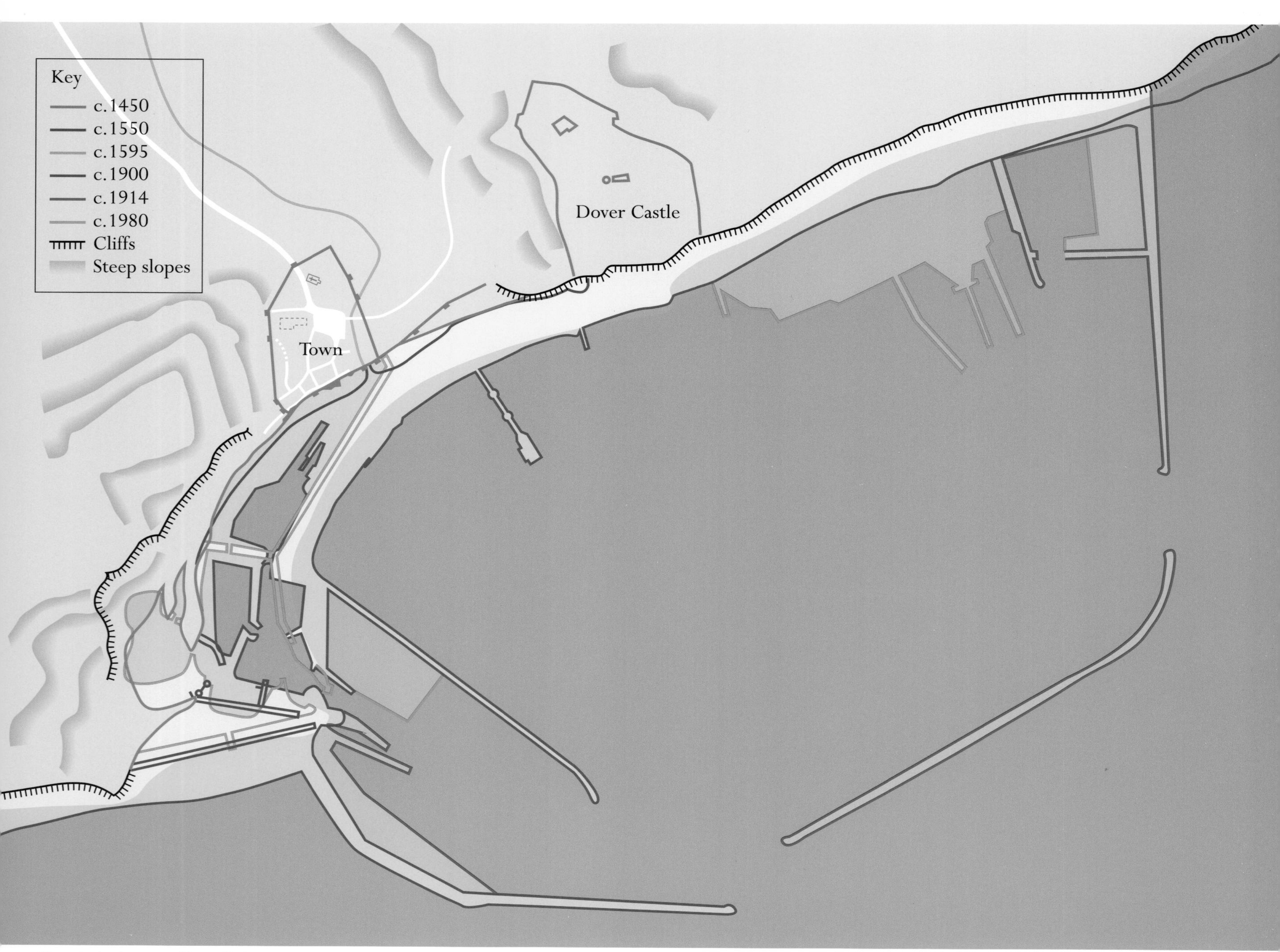


The main developments of Dover Harbour

# Introduction

This book celebrates the 400th anniversary of the Dover Harbour Board, first instituted by King James I in 1606. It did not, however, mark the beginning of Dover's harbour. As the nearest point in England to the continent of Europe and with the only break in its famous white cliffs, Dover and its harbour have played an important part in the nation's history by providing the most convenient place of entry and departure for this island, for both friends and foes, from the earliest times to the present day.

The strategic importance of this gateway in times of war and for communication and commerce in times of peace has long been recognised by the British monarchy and governments. This explains why, over the centuries, the royal family has not only made great use of Dover's harbour but has also taken a keen interest in its maintenance and development. It is appropriate, therefore, that this commemorative book focuses on visits to the harbour by the British royal family and upon its development from a crude safe haven to the modern bridge to Europe that it provides for Britain today.

These two themes are presented chronologically, but are differentiated so that readers may choose, if they wish, to follow only one theme; although, at times, the fortunes of the monarchy and the harbour are intertwined. It is hoped, however, that this fascinating story of Dover's harbour and its royal connections will be read in its entirety.

**Derek Leach**

Chapter 1 Early Days

*'The sea was confined by mountains so close to it that a dart could be thrown from their summit upon the shore.'* Julius Caesar 55BC

An impression of the Roman Fortress and settlement at Dover

The ornate and illuminated first letter of Jacobus (James ) begins the 1606 Royal Charter

By Royal Charter dated 6 October 1606 responsibility for Dover's harbour was placed in the hands of 'eleven discreet men' known as the Warden and Assistants of the Harbour of Dover. Headed by the Lord Warden of the Cinque (pronounced 'sink') Ports, there were only two local men – the serving Lieutenant Governor of Dover Castle and the serving mayor of Dover. The rest were courtiers appointed for life to this sinecure.

This was by no means the beginning of the story of Dover Harbour. From time immemorial a haven at Dover had been important for trade with the continent only 20 miles across the Channel, as a base for ships to defend the country from attack and for kings and princes journeying to the continent to make war, to negotiate peace or to seek a bride. The first recorded description of Dover and its bay was by Julius Caesar in 55BC when he tried to land, 'The sea was confined by mountains so close to it that a dart could be thrown from their summit upon the shore.'

Bronze Age boat on display in the Dover Museum

The valley between the high white cliffs was settled long before the Roman invasion in 43 AD. The exciting discovery of the Bronze Age Boat in 1992, buried six metres below the streets of Dover, indicates that sea-going craft were crossing the Channel and putting into this haven about 3,600 years ago. The River Dour rises just seven miles inland before flowing into the sea at what the Romans called Dubris, the Saxons called Dwyffra and we now call Dover. The Dour estuary was a valuable haven for the Romans. Archaeologists have found the remains of the harbour they constructed close to the present Market Square. On the cliffs on both sides of the valley the Romans built lighthouses to guide their ships into port, one of which can still be seen today alongside the church of Saint Mary-in-Castro – said to be one of the finest surviving Roman monuments in western Europe. The Roman occupation of Britain ended early in the fifth century and was followed by invasions by the Jutes, the Saxons and the Danes.

The burning of Dover
(Bayeux Tapestry)

## Norman invasion

The death in 1066 of the last Saxon king, Edward the Confessor, led to the Norman invasion. Duke William of Normandy had been in Dover previously on his way to see Edward, but his next visit in 1066 was as a conqueror, burning Dover in the process. Without an heir, Edward had apparently promised the throne to Duke William of Normandy but on his deathbed Earl Godwin's son, Harold, was chosen instead. William decided to take his inheritance by force, landed on the Sussex coast and defeated the Saxon army at the Battle of Hastings, during which Harold was killed and William the Conqueror, as he is now called, became king. After subduing England, William passed through Dover many times en route from his Normandy possessions.

Bayeaux Tapestry depiction
of the Battle of Hastings

A Cinque Ports ship ready for battle with its three castles in place

Cinque Ports' Barons at Henry VI's coronation in 1399

# The Cinque Ports

Many years before, the Saxon king, Alfred, who died in 1037, had demonstrated the need for supremacy at sea when fighting the Danes and eventually five south-east ports, Dover, Sandwich, Hythe, New Romney and Hastings, were grouped into a federation to provide ships and men for such a purpose – the Cinque (pronounced 'sink') Ports. Later, the two 'antient towns' of Winchelsea and Rye were added. The obligations of the Cinque Ports to the Crown were laid down in Saxon charters recorded in Domesday Book for William the Conqueror in 1086. William confirmed the arrangements. In return for various privileges, such as honours at court – including the right to carry a canopy over the monarch at coronations and to sit next to the monarch at the associated feasts – exemption from the king's taxes and the right to govern themselves, owing allegiance only to the king, the Cinque Ports had to supply the king with 57 ships once a year. Dover's contribution was 20 ships for 15 days with 21 men in each vessel. This could be for carrying the king across the Channel, or for military purposes transporting an army, or as a temporary naval fighting force. For the rest of the year these same ships went about their peacefu business of fishing and 'working the Passage' as carrying goods and travellers across the Channel was called. This organisation was at the height of its powers at the beginning of the 14th century, but began to decline with the birth of a proper Royal Navy. Today, of the original seven only Dover remains a major port.

Common seal of the Barons of Dover 1305

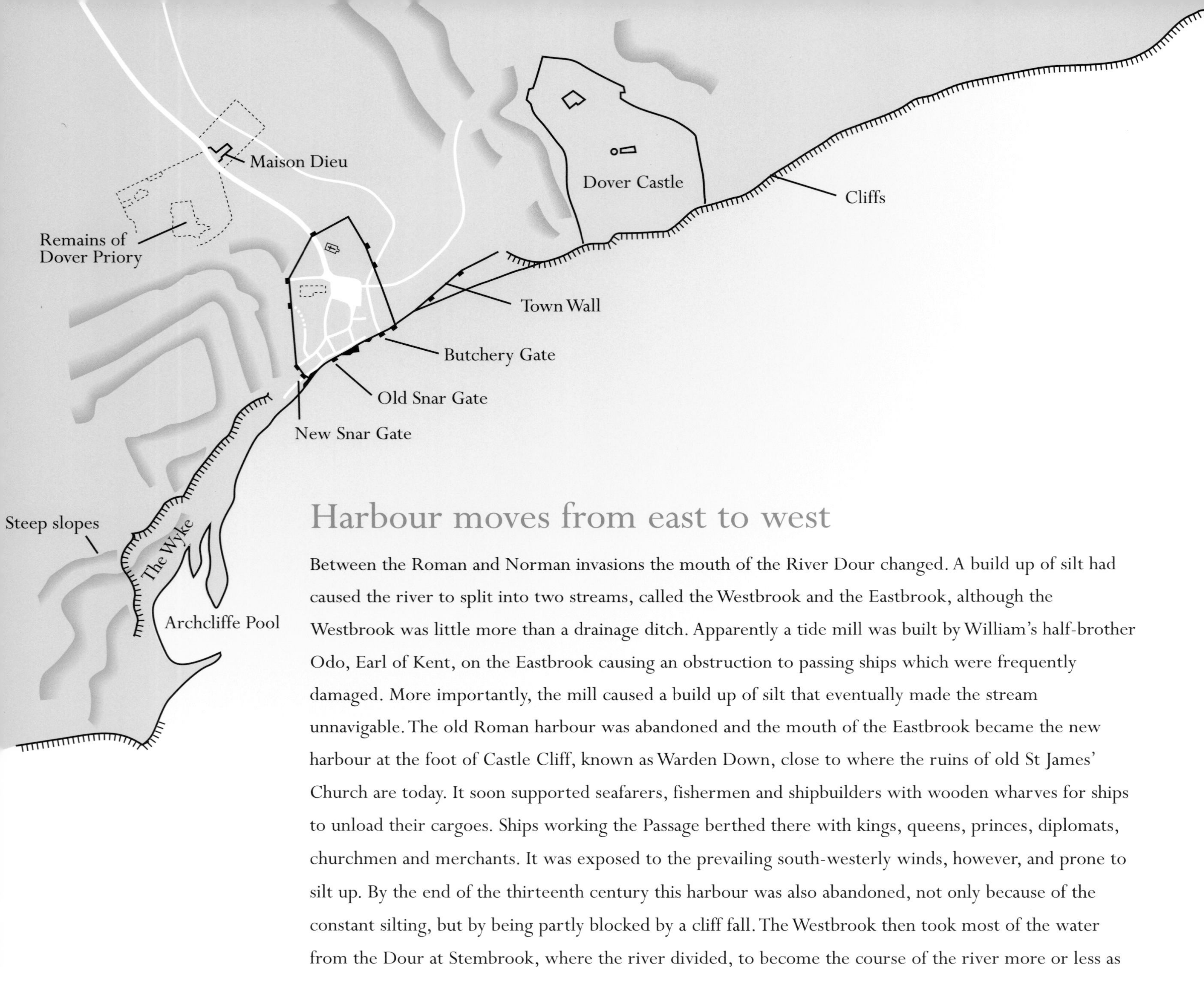


## Harbour moves from east to west

Between the Roman and Norman invasions the mouth of the River Dour changed. A build up of silt had caused the river to split into two streams, called the Westbrook and the Eastbrook, although the Westbrook was little more than a drainage ditch. Apparently a tide mill was built by William's half-brother Odo, Earl of Kent, on the Eastbrook causing an obstruction to passing ships which were frequently damaged. More importantly, the mill caused a build up of silt that eventually made the stream unnavigable. The old Roman harbour was abandoned and the mouth of the Eastbrook became the new harbour at the foot of Castle Cliff, known as Warden Down, close to where the ruins of old St James' Church are today. It soon supported seafarers, fishermen and shipbuilders with wooden wharves for ships to unload their cargoes. Ships working the Passage berthed there with kings, queens, princes, diplomats, churchmen and merchants. It was exposed to the prevailing south-westerly winds, however, and prone to silt up. By the end of the thirteenth century this harbour was also abandoned, not only because of the constant silting, but by being partly blocked by a cliff fall. The Westbrook then took most of the water from the Dour at Stembrook, where the river divided, to become the course of the river more or less as we know it today. With no harbour, ships had to be beached on the west side of the bay where some shelter was provided by a small promontory called Archcliffe.

Henry I and Queen Matilda

# Henry I and Stephen

Despite these problems, Henry I, who became king in 1100, used Dover and the Cinque Ports' ships to carry him and his army across the Channel to regain control of his continental lands. Henry was the third surviving son of William the Conqueror, but took the English crown when his brother, William II died. His elder brother Robert, Duke of Normandy, disputed this and the war of succession lasted until 1106 when Henry captured Robert and conquered Normandy. Many of his actions were morally dubious; even his 20 acknowledged illegitimate children were used in marriage alliances for the well-being of the state.

Henry I lost his son and heir in a Channel disaster in 1120. Henry and his son William, aged 16, were returning from France. Henry and the royal fleet left Barfleur ahead of his young son who followed in a separate ship. William, acting like a typical teenager perhaps, urged his crew to beat his father's vessel to Dover, but the ship struck rocks and sank. William, with many others on board, was drowned. It is said that Henry never smiled again.

Before Henry I died he made it known that he wanted his daughter Matilda (or Maud as she was sometimes known) to succeed him, relying upon his nephew, Stephen, to support her, but Stephen decided to seize the English throne for himself and landed at Dover in December 1135. The citizens of Dover refused to welcome him and he was not allowed to enter the castle. Undeterred he travelled on and seized the crown. A year later, Stephen's wife who had remained in Normandy, landed at Dover before she and Stephen were crowned in Canterbury Cathedral. Stephen returned only once to Normandy, in 1137. Matilda and her son, Henry, landed at Dover in 1139 with mercenaries and occupied the castle until peace was made. Stephen died in (the new) Dover Priory in 1154 at the end of a disastrous reign during which the country had been divided by a civil war with neither side securing complete control.

Thomas Becket

Eleanor of Aquitaine

## Henry II and Thomas Becket

Henry succeeded Stephen as Henry II and frequently called upon the services of the Cinque Ports' ships. This man of boundless energy had married Eleanor of Aquitaine when he was 19 years old and her duchy became part of his extensive dominions. This meant that he was a frequent cross-Channel traveller. In 1155 Henry II stayed at Dover Castle on his return from the continent. Henry II is perhaps best known in connection with the murder of Archbishop Thomas Becket in 1170. Earlier in the year Henry passed through Dover on his way to make peace with his exiled archbishop. Later, four knights from his court in Normandy crossed the Channel to Dover and butchered the archbishop in his own cathedral at Canterbury, believing that they were carrying out the King's wishes.

Richard I

## Richard I

With important dominions in France, the Norman and Plantagenet kings of England made great use of Dover, often staying at the castle awaiting favourable winds for France. King Richard I, Henry II's third son, known as 'the Lionheart,' came to Dover in 1189, stayed at the castle and sailed on 11 December for the Third Crusade with 100 large ships and 80 galleys. The crusades were military expeditions authorised by the Pope against people identified as enemies of the Church – particularly Muslims in the Middle East. Those who joined the crusades believed that they would receive a spiritual reward. Despite victories over Saladin, this fine soldier, Richard, failed to take Jerusalem and negotiated terms with Saladin in 1192. He did not return to England until 1194, because he was seized on his way home by Leopold of Austria in 1192 and then held to ransom until 1194 when he was released on payment of 34 tons of silver – equivalent to about three times the king's annual income!

King John

Magna Carta

# John

John succeeded his brother, Richard I, in 1199. He was unpopular and was opposed by the Pope, most of England's bishops and many of the great barons. It was the barons who forced John to sign Magna Carta, the famous charter of English liberties, at Runnymede in 1215. During his feud with the Pope over who should be archbishop of Canterbury, John came to Dover in 1210 to meet Stephen Langton, the Pope's choice, but Stephen refused to sail from France. The quarrel with the Pope rumbled on and John met Pandolph, the papal legate, in 1213 at Temple Ewell, three miles outside Dover in an attempt to end the feud. He met Pandolph again, later that year, in Dover and submitted to papal authority. A year later the Cinque Ports' ships took John and his army from Dover to France where he suffered a humiliating defeat. Worse was to come. In 1216 he faced an invasion force led by Louis, son of the King of France. He attempted to raise mercenaries to oppose Louis and his own rebellious barons, but failed. Louis landed and laid siege to Dover Castle, but was eventually repelled.

# Henry III

Henry III, eldest son of King John, succeeded his father in 1216, when only nine years old, with the country torn apart by his father's misrule. The King granted Dover the monopoly of carrying passengers to and from the continent in 1227. Involved in various half-hearted campaigns to recover lands in Europe lost by his father, he and his queen, with a thousand horsemen, stayed at Dover Castle in 1255 on his return from the continent. Despite being defeated and captured during the Barons War and temporarily dethroned, he managed to end his life as king.

Henry III

King Edward I crowned

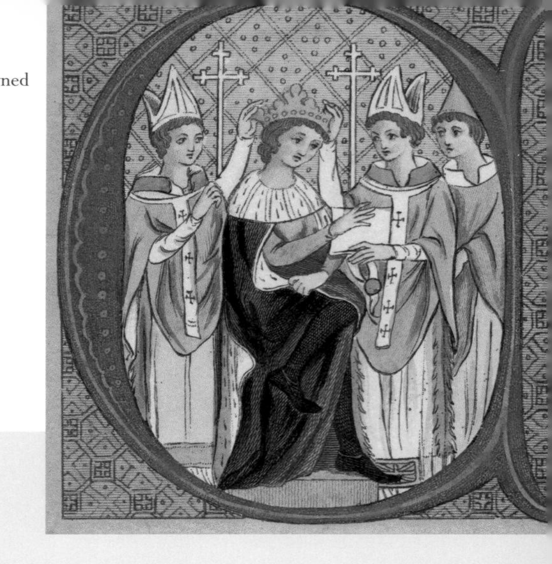

# Edward I

Edward I, whilst still heir to his father, Henry III, went on crusade to the Holy Land in 1270 and was wounded during an assassination attempt. On his way home during 1272 he heard of his father's death, but did not land in Dover until 2 August 1274. Like his predecessors he made great use of Dover's castle and haven. In 1297 he sailed for Flanders in the Cinque Ports' fleet to attack Philip of France. It was he who, having conquered Wales, set the precedent in 1301 of granting the principality to his eldest son and heir, naming him Prince of Wales.

# The handsomest pair in the world

Edward II was the fourteenth and last child of Edward I and Eleanor of Castile. Described as 'fair of body and great of strength,' he lacked brains! Another frequent royal visitor, he issued his coronation proclamation from Dover Castle. In 1308 after staying overnight at the castle, he sailed for France to marry the French king's daughter known as 'Isobel the Fair'. With his good looks they were known as 'the handsomest pair in the world.' His queen was sent to France in 1324 to discuss peace terms with her brother, Charles IV. This was a disaster because she refused to return to England and, instead, invaded in 1326. Edward abdicated in favour of his 14 year old son, Edward III, and died in prison, probably the victim of a gruesome murder ordered by his lovely wife.

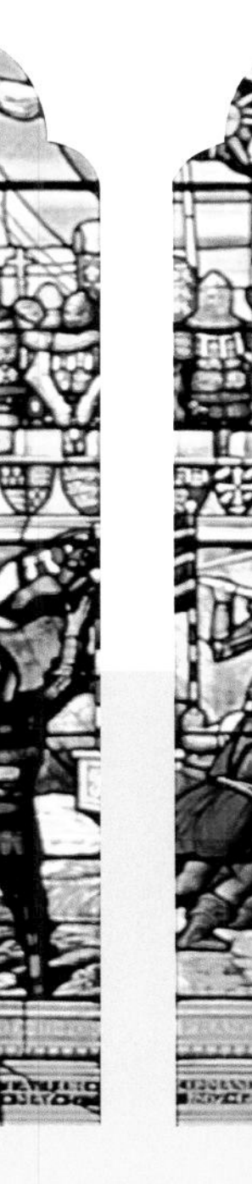

Embarkation of Edward III at Dover in 1359 depicted in a stained glass window in the Maison Dieu, Dover

## Start of the Hundred Years War

Edward III visited Dover twice early in 1329 en route for, and then returning from, paying homage to the French king for Edward's dominions in France. He and his queen visited the French king again in 1331. The good folk of Dover were grateful to King Edward when, in 1336, he decreed that all merchants, travellers and pilgrims crossing the Channel had to use Dover. Another visit in 1364 was to arrange a marriage between the Earl of Flanders' daughter and Edmund, Duke of Cambridge. Tension over the status of Aquitaine had led to wars with the French in 1294-1303 and 1324-26, but Edward III's long reign saw renewal of the conflict in 1337, which became known as the Hundred Years War. This was aggravated in 1340 when Edward formally assumed the title 'King of France.' Once again Dover's haven and castle were busy with the comings and goings of the King, his son the Black Prince and their armies, winning the Battle of Crecy in 1346 and in the following year besieging and taking Calais. It was Edward III who instituted the Order of the Garter, comprising 26 companions plus the sovereign, as a celebration of the campaign with its motto, 'Honi soit qui mal y pense.' The Order survives to this day as a symbol of the continuity of the monarchy.

The Garter

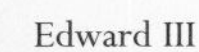

Edward III

Richard II

## Richard II

Anne of Bohemia

In 1377 the son of Edward the Black Prince became king as Richard II whilst still a boy and in 1382 Dover welcomed him and his queen, Anne of Bohemia, when they landed at Dover. He was very distraught when she died in 1394. Nevertheless, there was a political need to remarry and in 1396 he left Dover for France, returning with his new bride, Isobel of Valois, who was only eight years old. Needless to say, this was not a love match. Immortalised in Shakespeare's play, *Richard II*, he was deposed in 1399 and murdered by Henry IV. In 1402 his young widow was sent back to France via Dover in disgrace.

## Henry V and Agincourt

Following Henry IV's early death in 1413, his son Henry V, another object of Shakespeare's pen, succeeded him and decided to exercise his right, by battle if necessary, to the crown of France. After leaving Dover with 6,500 horsemen and 21,000 foot soldiers, he besieged Honfleur for six weeks before taking it. On St. Crispin's Day, 25 October, 1415 this born warrior, outnumbered six to one, won the famous battle of Agincourt and became a hero overnight. This enabled Henry to conquer Normandy and he returned to Dover in triumph. With him were captive French nobles held to ransom, but also the bodies of the Duke of York and the Earl of Norfolk. Ivan Green, in his book *Dover and The Monarchy* wrote, 'In 1415 Henry V sailed with his army from Dover and fought and won the great battle of Agincourt, afterwards recognised as a masterpiece of strategy of a small force against a much larger one. His skilful use of the 300 Kentish bowmen contributed greatly to the success of the campaign. News of his great victory reached Dover before his return and Lingard relates how the crowd plunged into the waves to meet him and the conqueror was carried in their arms from his vessel to the beach.'

In the following year the Pope tried to make peace between England and France, sending Sigismund, King of Rome, to England as a mediator. His reception at Dover was peculiar. Henry had sent 30 Cinque Ports' ships to bring him across the Channel, but when the ships approached the shore the Duke of Gloucester, who was the Lord Warden and the King's brother, with many knights rode into the sea with drawn swords and, on the instructions of the King, stated that Sigismund could only land if he was coming as a peace mediator and not to claim any jurisdiction in England. Having confirmed that this was so, Sigismund landed with all honours! The King made a favourable impression on him and at a subsequent conference in Calais a treaty was drawn up acknowledging Henry's claim to the French throne.

Despite this, Henry led a second army to France in 1417. For five years enthusiastic parliaments voted him all the money he needed and no French army dared stand in his way. The French king recognised him as his heir and in 1421 Henry landed at Dover with his bride, the beautiful Catherine of Valois, daughter of the French king. Soon after the coronation of his queen, his brother, the Duke of Clarence and governor of Normandy, was slain in a revolt against the English. Henry returned to France with a force of 26,000 including many bowmen in 500 ships. Before the end of the year the English were masters of the north of France and Henry established himself in Paris. He never became King of France, however, as he died at the height of his triumphs at the age of 35 in 1422, a few weeks before the death of his father-in-law. Henry's body was landed at Dover. The town mourned for its great King as the long procession, including the King of Scotland, wound its way through the narrow streets on its way to London, headed by 500 men at arms in black armour, accompanied by muffled drums, priests chanting on either side of the coffin, the Barons of the Cinque Ports carrying a canopy above it and with his queen at the rear. So, a very lucrative business for Dover, transporting soldiers to France, came to an end, at least for the time being.

In the Temple gardens, London, the Duke of York picks a white rose, the Duke of Lancaster prefers the red… and so a legend is born and a nasty war gets a pretty name

## Wars of the Roses

His son, Henry VI, became King of England at the age of nine months and was also proclaimed King of France in accordance with the peace treaty. This Henry only visited his continental kingdom once, in 1430-32, when still a boy. He did not enjoy the success of his father for it was during his reign that all the English lands in France were lost, except for Calais. There was a happy occasion when he brought back from Calais to Dover his bride, Margaret of Anjou, in 1445. She turned out to be a domineering woman, however, who overwhelmed the King and increased the opposition to him. It was a tragic reign as England slid into civil war, the Wars of the Roses, when the rival Houses of York and Lancaster fought for possession of the crown. Henry himself was murdered in 1471 and his queen, who had crossed the Channel several times to bolster the Lancastrian cause, fled to her father in Provence. In 1475 Edward IV sailed from Dover to Calais with his great army, said to be of 30,000 men, in 500 ships to help his brother in law, Charles of Burgundy against Louis XI of France. Peace was made without an arrow being fired and Edward returned to Dover with his army.

The 8-year old Henry VI receives the 'sacre' (coronation) in Paris, by way of emphasising England's claim to much French territory

Lancastrian Henry VII, the first of the Tudor kings, brought to an end the Wars of the Roses by marrying Elizabeth of York, Edward IV's daughter. He crossed the Channel with his army to France in 1492 and gained a profitable peace. He liked Dover and made the castle his home on several occasions. Henry VII's decree that English goods should be carried in English ships helped the moribund Dover fleet to become prosperous again and led to new warehouses springing up round its little harbour. When he died in 1509 he left his son, Henry VIII, a peaceful and united realm at last.

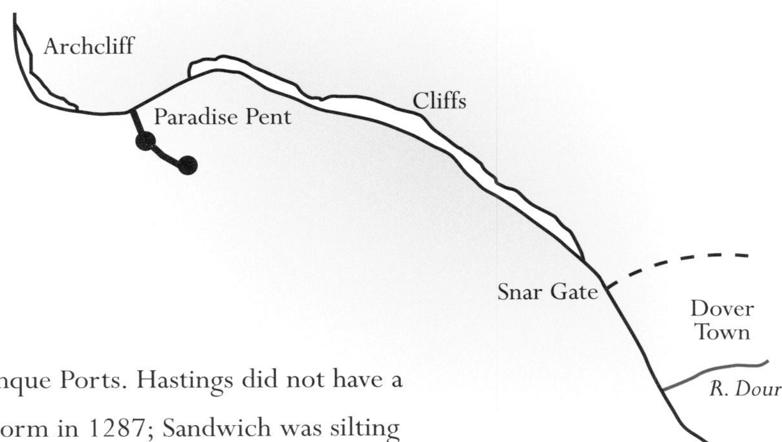


## Clark's harbour improvements

Dependence upon Dover increased with the decay of the other Cinque Ports. Hastings did not have a proper harbour anyway; Winchelsea had been abandoned after a storm in 1287; Sandwich was silting up; Romney had been cut off from the sea in the fourteenth century. Dover's little natural shelter at Archcliffe, where mud and shingle had formed a pool open to the sea, allowed ships to berth in safety protected from the prevailing winds. Despite these advantages it was not adequate for the main arrival and departure point for the continent. Improvements were necessary.

The first attempt at improvement was made in 1495 by Sir John Clark, a priest and master of the Maison Dieu. This was a religious house founded in 1203 by Hubert de Burgh, Constable of Dover Castle, which gave shelter to pilgrims on their way to Becket's tomb in Canterbury Cathedral and which was also a hospital. The impressive main building still stands in Dover and is used as the town hall. On the seaward side of the pool Clark built a jetty, with a tower at one end, made of chalk and filled with earth. The haven so created was so successful, for a while, that it was called Paradise. Shingle accumulated on the seaward side and strengthened it; however, the shingle soon crept round the end of the jetty and threatened to block the harbour mouth. The jetty was extended with another tower on the end to narrow the harbour mouth.

Henry VIII

Henry VIII's Armour

# Henry VIII

Henry VIII, remembered primarily for his break with the Pope, his dissolution of the monasteries and for his six wives, spent a great deal of time in the town and took a great interest in its harbour and defences. His father had appointed him Lord Warden and Constable of Dover Castle in 1483. Henry embarked on the traditional source of royal glory – several expensive wars with France. On 15 June 1513 he arrived at Dover Castle with his queen, Catherine of Aragon, and ordered the Cinque Ports to fit out its fleet to take him and his army to France. After 15 days he sailed on 30 June and won a great victory over the French, known as the Battle of the Spurs because of the speed of the French retreat. Peace with France followed in 1514 and as part of the treaty Henry agreed that his younger sister, Mary, should marry the French king. Mary, with Anne Boleyn as a maid of honour, came to Dover en route for France. Bad weather kept her for a whole month in Dover Castle before she could sail to France for her wedding.

Catherine of Aragon, daughter of Ferdinand and Isabella of Spain, first Queen of Henry VIII

Harbour during Henry VIII's reign

Henry VIII embarking from Clark's Pier for Field of Cloth of Gold, 1520

# Field of Cloth of Gold

In 1520 Henry rode into Dover at the head of a great torchlight procession to welcome the Holy Roman Emperor, Charles V, when he landed at Dover. He was the eldest son of the queen's sister. Clark's jetty was still intact when, later that year, Henry VIII and his queen, Catherine of Aragon, sailed for what became known as the Field of Cloth of Gold in France. Henry stayed at Dover Castle whilst his enormous retinue of 500 horsemen and 3,000 on foot assembled. Provisions for a month were ordered, '700 quarters of wine, 150 tuns of French wine, 6 butts of sweet wine, 560 tuns of beer, 340 beeves at 40 shillings, 4,200 muttons at 5 shillings, 80 hogsheads of grease, salt and fresh fish £30, spices £440, diapers £300, 4,000 pounds of candles £26.13s.4d, poultry £1,300, pewter vessels £300, pans and spits £200, 5,600 quarters of coal, tallwood and billets £200, sables £200.' It must have been quite a party! The political purpose of the meeting in France between Henry and Francis I was to reinforce the 1518 treaty of perpetual friendship between England and France and the associated marriage alliance between the

Man-of-War in which Henry VIII embarked in 1520 to go to France

Anne Boleyn

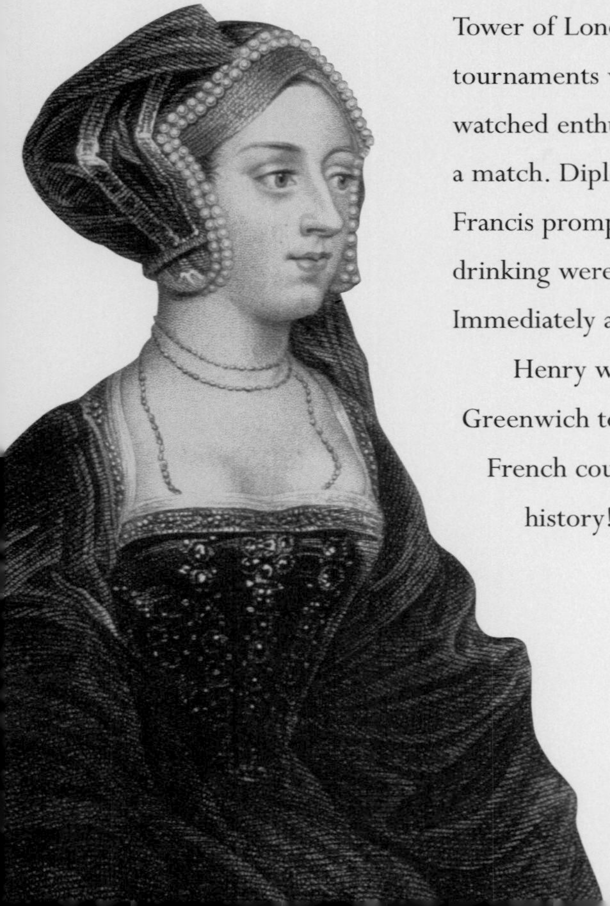

Dauphin aged 20 months, the heir to the French throne, and Henry's daughter Mary, then aged two and a half! The setting was in the 'golden vale' between the village of Guines within the English Calais province and Ardres in France. Even though it might mean bankruptcy, the two kings competed in magnificence and extravagance. This lavish meeting lasted seventeen days, taking the form of a series of splendid tournaments. The two kings met in a tent of cloth of gold provided by Henry. A large palace was constructed of brick and timber, painted to look like stone. The walls were 38 feet high. Some of it had been constructed in England and shipped across the Channel. Needless to say, the interior was lavishly furnished and decorated, a superb example of English craftsmanship. The tournament field had spectator galleries and triumphal arches. Swords were made on site and 1,000 spear staves were sent from the Tower of London. Challenges were sent all over Europe, but only England and France took part! These tournaments were preceded by elaborate ceremonies and processions. The two kings did not joust, but watched enthusiastically. There is a story told that Henry liked to wrestle and would invite his courtiers to a match. Diplomatically, they would always let Henry win, but when Henry challenged the French king, Francis promptly trounced him! However, Henry beat him at archery. Needless to say, the feasting and drinking were endless. Designed to end hostilities between the two countries, it was all in vain. Immediately after the meeting Francis refortified Ardres with wood from Henry's pavilion!

Henry was in Dover again in 1522 to meet Emperor Charles V when he landed. They took ship to Greenwich to meet Queen Catherine. War with France was renewed and Anne Boleyn returned from the French court via Dover and was appointed maid of honour to the queen – and the rest, they say, is history! By 1532 Anne was living openly with the King, but not yet his wife or queen when they visited King Francis I in Calais. These royal arrivals and departures were often accompanied by lavish festivities in the castle and town. Such an occasion was when Anne of Cleves arrived at Dover in 1539 to become Henry VIII's fourth wife. She was expected before Christmas, but the weather was so bad that she was forced to spend it in Calais. On 27 December she sailed for Dover with 50 ships, but landed at Deal and was then conducted to Dover Castle.

Field of Cloth of Gold

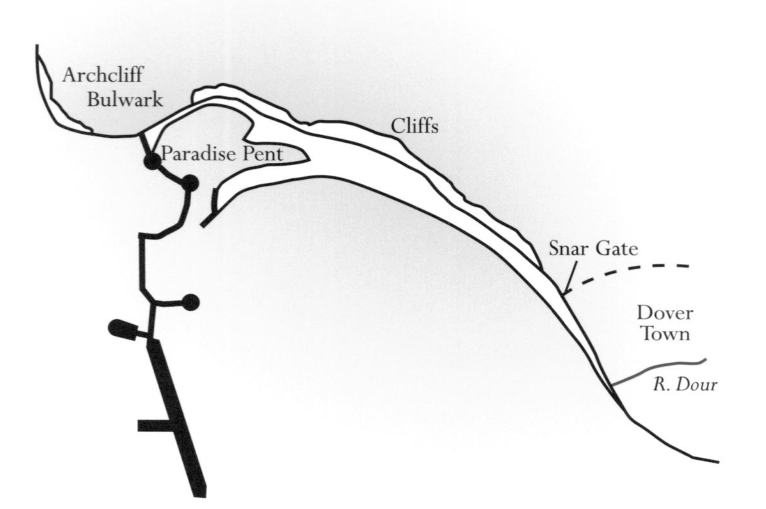

Harbour in 1535 after Thompson's improvements

# Thompson's harbour improvements

By 1530, most of Clark's pier had been destroyed by gales and the harbour was gradually being choked by shingle. Another clergyman, Sir John Thompson, minister of old St. James' Church, presented plans for improvement to the authorities in the town which were received enthusiastically. £300 was sought from King Henry VIII for the work, which was granted. Thompson was appointed engineer and work began in 1533 on a new and longer pier, 770 feet long, to deflect shingle past the harbour mouth. It was much more solid than Clark's jetty with two parallel rows of piles driven into the sea bed, bound together and infilled with chalk. More money as required was made available by the King and Henry took great interest in it, visiting the work several times. As a reward, Thompson was appointed master of the Maison Dieu by Henry VIII.

The new pier looked impressive, but lacked a good flow of water from a river to shift the ever increasing shingle at the harbour mouth. Thompson tried again and built a separate mole in deeper water. It was very expensive and having spent £60,000 on it, Henry cut off funds and the unfinished work was left to the elements.

# Henry VIII's defences

In 1539, following Henry VIII's break with the Roman Catholic Church, England was in danger of being invaded by France and Spain, encouraged by the Pope. Henry launched a programme of defence building around the east and south coasts including castles at Deal, Walmer and Sandgate to the east and west of Dover. At Dover he built three gun positions to deter any landings in Dover Bay. Two of these survive today – Archcliffe Fort at the western end of the bay and Mote's Bulwark halfway up the castle cliff.
The Cinque Ports' ships took Henry and an army to France for the last time in 1544, where he had mixed success, although he did capture Boulogne after a fierce siege and returned to Dover with its gates!
This was the last time he had personal contact with Dover before dying in 1547.

Edward VI

## Edward VI's charter

By 1556 Paradise harbour was useless to shipping, although ships tied up to the remnants of the piers. Edward VI, son of Henry VIII, granted the town a charter confirming a monopoly of the Channel crossing. Later, Queen Mary, Edward VI's sister, allowed the mayor of Dover to beg money throughout the country for its harbour. Nevertheless, this monopoly was ignored by other Kent ports and the whole country ignored the begging bowl!

## Queen Mary's charter

A fundamental problem was the landing of goods and passengers from ships forced to anchor offshore with many small boats employed to ferry passengers and goods to and from the beach. Operators of these boats were completely uncontrolled and charged exorbitant fees. Queen Mary granted a charter to the town in 1553 designed to give the town powers to control them:

Queen Mary

'Know that we of our special grace and of our certain knowledge and mere motion have given and granted, and by these presents do give and grant, to our beloved Mayor, Jurats and Commonalty of our town of Dover, in our county of Kent, the ravage and ferriage of our whole port of Dover in our said county of Kent, from all manner of skiffs and boats within the port aforesaid for the carrying of men and other things to be carried and transported from the shore of the port aforesaid to the ships in the aforesaid port, and lying at anchor to the deep sea near the aforesaid port, and from those ships to the shore aforesaid so that none there presume to convey or transport any thing or any men in any skiffs, vessels or boats, except only in the boats or vessels of the inhabitants of our said town of Dover, without the licence of the said Mayor, Jurats and Commonalty….'

## Good Queen Bess

Elizabeth, daughter of Henry VIII and Anne Boleyn, became queen in 1558 and reigned for 45 years. During the 1570s Elizabeth toured the country showing herself to her people and in 1573 she began her great progress through Kent, riding on horseback most of the way. She was met by the Archbishop of Canterbury en route and the Queen so admired his horse that he felt obliged to offer it to her as a gift, which she promptly accepted! So great was her entourage that apparently when she reached Dover the tail end of her procession was still climbing the hill out of Folkestone seven miles away. By the time the Queen arrived in Dover she was tired and brought the mayor's long welcoming speech to an abrupt halt with, 'Most gracious fool, get off that stool!'

At this time Dover's harbour was in great difficulty, being continually blocked by shingle. Only ships drawing less than four feet of water could pass the harbour entrance compared with ships drawing 20 feet in Henry VIII's time. During Elizabeth's six day stay at Dover Castle the mayor of Dover took advantage of her visit to petition her about the state of the harbour. An investigation was ordered into the state of harbours round the Kent coast – why they had decayed, how best to repair them and which would be best for the future. Dover won this 'top port' contest when the commission reported, 'how needful for this realm such a haven is in that place, which is at the point where the seas are narrowest, and may for the apt situation thereof be accounted as one of the eyes of our country.' Despite these fine words, nothing came of it.

This did not prevent William Borough, who had been chairman of the commission, from drawing up several memoranda, describing the cause of the decay of Paradise harbour, suggesting a new harbour protected at its mouth by two jetties with a large pool of pent up water, which could be released at times through sluices to clear the shingle away from the harbour entrance. A consultation meeting in Dover in 1579 welcomed the scheme, but not the £18,200 estimated cost!

Queen Elizabeth I painted in 1598 to hang in the town hall at Dover

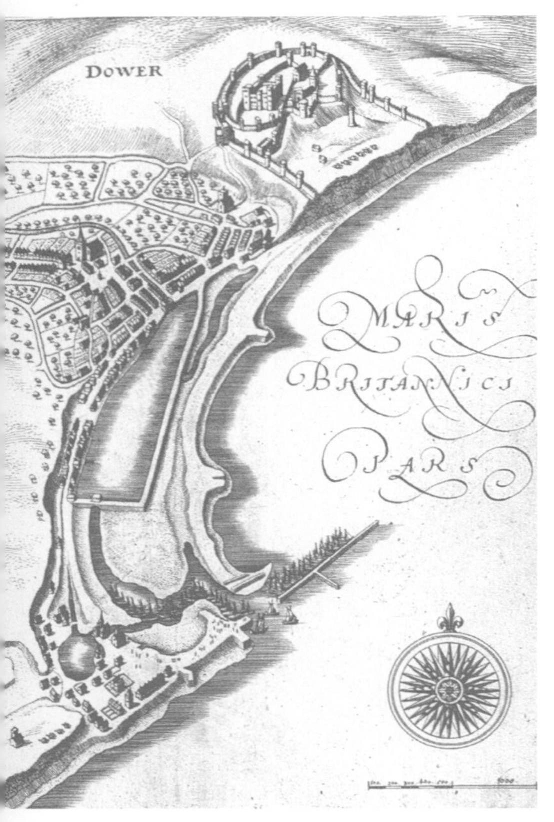


Harbour in Elizabeth's reign

## Passing Tolls Act and Thomas Digges

A document produced by a local man, Thomas Digges, who was a mathematician, land surveyor and member of parliament, on how to build Borough's harbour triggered another enquiry in 1581. Valuable support came from Sir Walter Raleigh who stressed the need for a safe anchorage at Dover both for trade and naval purposes. Consequently, Queen Elizabeth approved the Act of Passing Tolls, levying a tax on all ships above a certain tonnage entering or leaving the country. The proceeds were for harbour construction at Dover.

John True was appointed at 10 shillings a day to supervise the construction of a long stone wall, running parallel to the shore against the huge bank of shingle that had built up, to the harbour mouth where a crosswall with sluices in it would run to the shore. The River Dour would empty into this pool of water and be released through the sluices to flush away the obstructing shingle. Little progress was made despite money being spent and True was replaced by a Dutch engineer, Ferdinand Poins, who did no better and was also dismissed.

Finally, Thomas Digges was appointed. He proposed an even more ambitious plan, which would enclose Dover Bay from the shore by Woolcomber Street (where the Leisure Centre is now) to Archcliffe with an opening for this new harbour near what is now New Bridge. Land reclaimed by the pier at Paradise and under Castle Cliff could be leased for building, raising money to maintain the harbour. Something similar did eventually happen centuries later, but it was far too ambitious for Digges' time. He was forced to concentrate upon True's plan, which he simplified. One shilling a day was offered to each man with a horse and cart. As many as 1,000 men and 500 carts were employed, delivering local materials to build the walls. Begun in 1583, the wall was half a mile long after three months and several feet above high water. The harbour formed was known as Great Paradise and the original Paradise was fitted with a wall and lock gates plus a sluice forcing water on to the shingle at the harbour mouth.

Henry IV, King of France

## Secret visit by Elizabeth

The second visit of Queen Elizabeth I to Dover in 1601 only two years before her death is not so well known. Whilst it is not known whether she visited the harbour, it was certainly a near miss! Unlike the pomp of 1573, she travelled in some secrecy with the sole purpose of trying to persuade Henry IV, King of France, to cross the Channel to talk about the balance of power in Europe and the threat from Austria. Much to her annoyance, Henry refused to come to Dover. He, in turn, suggested that Elizabeth should meet him in Calais. She refused and in a letter in her own hand wrote to Henry, regretting that because of their royal positions neither could be seen to meet in the other's lands. It was in Dover Castle that Elizabeth told Henry's minister that she wanted James VI of Scotland to be her heir. 'One day the King of Scotland will become the King of Great Britain,' she predicted and so he did. It was only on her deathbed that she told her own ministers of her wish.

Following the death of Elizabeth in 1603, no lasting solutions to the problems of Dover Harbour were produced. There were many reports and plans, but most were ignored. It took some time to realise that what was needed was a very long protective jetty to either side of the harbour entrance to send the shingle out into deep water on the western side and to provide protection from the easterly winds on the other. In any case, such long piers were not technically feasible until the nineteenth century.

# Chapter 2 1606-1861

*'I have thought the best I can of the place where I should disembark and have resolved, God willing, to land at Dover.'* Charles II, 15 May 1660

James I

## The Royal Charter of 1606

King James VI of Scotland, son of Mary, Queen of Scots, succeeded Elizabeth in 1603 to become James I of England. Harbour works had ceased and the Commissioners appointed to supervise them had resigned. Control returned to the Dover Corporation who received the harbour dues but did not spend them wisely. James, having survived the Gunpowder Plot of 1605, extended the Passing Tolls Act for another seven years, but appointed a committee to look into how the money was spent. The Earl of Northampton, who had the ear of the King, became Lord Warden of the Cinque Ports in 1604 and complained about the Corporation's management of the harbour. The committee's conclusions were a bombshell for the Corporation. James demanded that Dover Corporation surrender control of the harbour. By royal charter dated 6 October 1606 management was vested in 'eleven discreet men' – the Lord Warden, the Lieutenant of the Castle, the Mayor of Dover during his year of office and eight courtiers, appointed for life, who apparently neither knew nor cared at all about harbours. They were known as the Guardian or Warden and Assistants of the Harbour of Dover. The Lord Warden did not attend meetings for more than a hundred years and so in practice the harbour was run by the Lieutenant of the Castle and the mayor, with or without the help of the courtiers – mainly without! Control of the port's affairs remained with this organisation until 1861. The town did manage to retain the right to license boatmen to land and embark passengers on the shore and the right of Dover's own ships to free harbourage.

This well-intentioned scheme brought little success with no great harbour works, only repairs and minor improvements. Paradise Pent slowly became a smelly marsh with the main harbour threatening to follow suit. The situation was so bad that, until 1676, townspeople turned out with shovels at the sound of a drum to clear the harbour mouth of shingle.

The royal charter also stipulated that any reclaimed land up to the cliffs below Snargate and along the shore as far as the castle, including land forming on the seaward side of the Pent, should belong to the Harbour Board. As land was reclaimed, houses were built upon it and more and more rent accrued to the Board.

## Charles I

Prince Charles, later Charles I, with his great friend the Duke of Buckingham, set sail from Dover in 1623 bound for Spain. It was supposed to be a secret trip with Charles calling himself John Smith, but the secret was not well kept and when he arrived in Dover he was welcomed by the Mayor and Corporation! Charles was hoping to make the Spanish Infanta his bride, but it came to nothing. Spurned, he returned to Dover later in the year.

King James I died in 1625 and Charles became king. He was already betrothed to Henrietta Maria, daughter of the French king, said to be the prettiest woman in France. They had met when he passed through Paris on his way to Madrid in 1623, when Henrietta had apparently remarked, 'The Prince of Wales need not have gone so far as Madrid to look for a wife.' After being very seasick during the ten hour voyage across the Channel to join Charles, she disembarked in relative comfort on a specially-built movable bridge from the shore. The town's porters carried her ashore on a litter and then she went by coach to Dover Castle to recover and to be welcomed by the mayor. The uncomfortable and dirty old castle had been made ready for her arrival, but she was unimpressed both by her welcome and the accommodation. King Charles arrived the next day from Canterbury to meet his 16 year old bride for the first time – they had been married by proxy already! They met on the grand staircase of the castle keep. She knelt at his feet and kissed his hand and then he took her in his arms and kissed her. Charles, having been told that Henrietta was petite as well as beautiful, was surprised that she was almost as tall as he, but Henrietta assured him that she was not wearing high heels! The marriage was solemnized at Canterbury Cathedral. People expected Charles to be a staunch protestant king, but his Catholic queen brought several Roman Catholic priests in her retinue of 400, all of whom were later banished from England.

Charles I

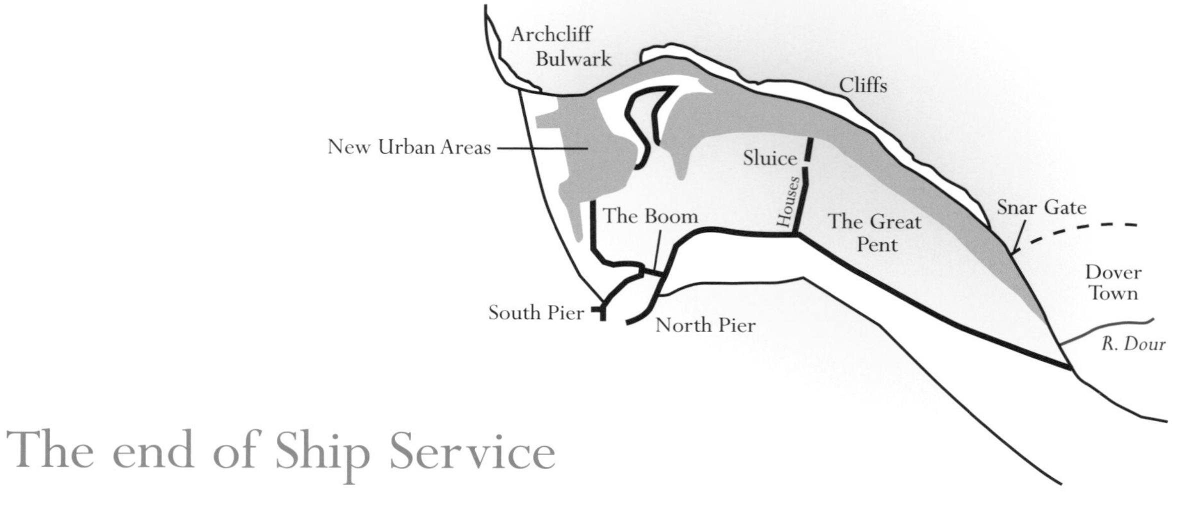


# The end of Ship Service

The end of an era came in 1626 when the town paid £482.10s to fund the ships of the Cinque Ports for three months, but it was the last time that Dover took any responsibility for the provision of ships. William Eldred's drawing of Dover Harbour in 1641 gives a good idea of what it looked like. Since 1585 the Pent crosswall had been widened sufficiently to allow houses to be built on it. Paradise Pent (or Little Paradise) was rapidly silting up with streets appearing around it – the beginnings of the Pier District.

# Civil War

By 1640 parliamentary opposition to King Charles was growing rapidly. Civil war followed. Queen Henrietta was busy trying to raise support for her husband in France and Holland. She crossed the Channel from Dover in 1640, taking with her the crown jewels for safekeeping. She returned, but on 23 February 1642 Charles I came to Dover to see the departure of his queen and his daughter, Princess Mary, when they left for Holland to raise men and munitions. Henrietta returned once again to England in 1643, landing in Yorkshire. Pregnant with her fifth child, the queen left the royal court at Oxford to have her child in a safer place. Henrietta Maria was born at Exeter in June. Charles never saw his wife again. She left Falmouth on 14 July 1644 for France. There is a story that later the same year, their baby daughter, Princess Henrietta, left behind when the queen escaped to France, also left for France disguised as a beggar boy. Charles I was captured in the Battle of Naseby later that year and was beheaded in 1649. Parliament then governed England without a king.

Queen Henrietta

Charles II lands at Dover

## The Restoration of Charles II

With the death of Oliver Cromwell in 1658, the country soon became disenchanted with the Commonwealth. Negotiations with Charles I's son, another Charles, in exile in Holland, led to an invitation to return to England as king in 1660. Dover featured in this historic event. On 15 May the King wrote to General Monk, 'I have thought the best I can of the place where I should disembark and have resolved, God willing, to land at Dover.' Two of the ships sent to Holland to bring the King back were commanded by Dover men. One of them, William Stokes, was master of the *Naseby*, the country's great new ship, which carried Charles and his entourage back to England. Charles immediately renamed the vessel *Royal Charles*. The splendid fleet sailed into Dover Bay on 25 May 1660, watched, it is said, by 50,000 people and carrying £50,000 – a gift from parliament to Charles. With the harbour once again blocked by shingle the King had to disembark on the beach. Apparently, the King's dog disgraced himself and used the landing boat as a lavatory, causing much amusement. The same Captain William Stokes was mayor of Dover 16 years later when a fine silver gilt mace was bought by the corporation with an inscription commemorating the landing and with a crowned head bearing the royal arms of the Stuarts. This famous landing at Dover was described in detail by Samuel Pepys, the diarist, who was with the royal party:

The scene is depicted in stained glass at the Maison Dieu, Dover

'By the morning we were close to the land, and everybody made ready to get on shore. The King and the two Dukes did eat their breakfast before they went, and there being set some ship's diet, they eat nothing else but pease and pork, and boiled beef. Dr. Clerke, who eat with me, told me how the King had given £50 to Mr Shepley for my Lord's servants, and £500 among the officers and common men of the ship. I spoke to the Duke of York about business, who called me Pepys by name, and upon my desire did promise me his future favour. Great expectations of the King making some Knights, but there was none. About noon he went in my Lord's barge with the two Dukes. Our Captain steered, and my Lord went along bare with him. I went, and Mr Mansell and one of the King's footmen, and a dog that the King loved, in a boat by ourselves, and so got on shore when the King did, who was received by General Monk with all imaginable love and respect at his entrance upon the land of Dover. Infinite the crowd of people and the horsemen, citizens and noblemen of all sorts. The mayor of the town come and gave him his white staffe, the badge of his place, which the King did give him again. The mayor also presented him from the town a very rich Bible, which he took and said it was the thing that he loved above all things in the world. A canopy was provided for him to stand under, which he did, and talked awhile with General Monk and others, and so into a stately coach there set for him, and so away through the towne towards Canterbury, without making any stay at Dover. The shouting and joy expressed by all is past imagination.' The handing of the mayor's staff to the sovereign was the usual tradition, signifying the town's subjection to the royal person and the handing back of it confirmed the mayor's authority and the town's loyalty.

Samuel Pepys
the famous diarist

Dover Corporation also recorded this memorable event, '....the King arrived in Dover Roads from Holland with twenty sail of His Majesty's great ships and frigates,

The King with
Lady Castlemaine
in party mood

the Right Hon. Edward Lord Montague being General, and landed the same day being attended by His Excellency the Lord General Monk who first met His Majesty upon the bridge let into the sea for His Majesty's more safe and convenient landing, and at His Majesty's coming from the bridge, the Mayor of this Town, Thomas Broome, Esq. made a speech to His Majesty upon his knees, and Mr. John Reading, Minister of the Gospel, presented His Majesty with the Holy Bible as a gift from this town, and Mr. Reading thereupon made a speech likewise to His Majesty and His Gracious Majesty laying his hand upon his breast, told Mr. Mayor nothing would be more dear to him than the Bible. His Excellency the Lord General was accompanied with the Earl of Winchilsea and a great number of nobility and gentry of England and his life guard all most richly accoutred.'

Apparently the deafening noise created by the saluting cannons meant that few heard this exchange of compliments. Charles returned in triumph to London where a thanksgiving service in Westminster Abbey was cancelled and Charles slipped away to spend the night with Barbara Palmer, soon to be Lady Castlemaine and a favourite of Charles. As a contemporary wit put it:

'Twelve years complete he suffered in exile
And kept his father's asses all the while
At length by wonderful impulse of Fate
The people call him home to help the State,
And what is more they send him money too,
And clothe him all from head to foot anew;
Nor did he such small favours then disdain,
But in his thirtieth year began to reign.
In a slashed doublet then he came to shore,
And dubbed poor Palmer's wife his Royal whore'.

## Return of Queen Henrietta

In October 1660 Charles I's widow, Queen Henrietta, returned to England with her daughter, Princess Henrietta, who was called Minette by the family. This was a joyful occasion with her escort of ships bedecked with flags as they reached Dover. Her son, Charles II, went on board to welcome them and later a banquet was held in the castle for the whole royal family.

Before long, Queen Henrietta and Minette returned to France where the princess married Philip, Duke of Orleans, the only brother of King Louis XIV. Although Queen Henrietta returned to England in 1662, she went back to France in 1665 where she spent her remaining years.

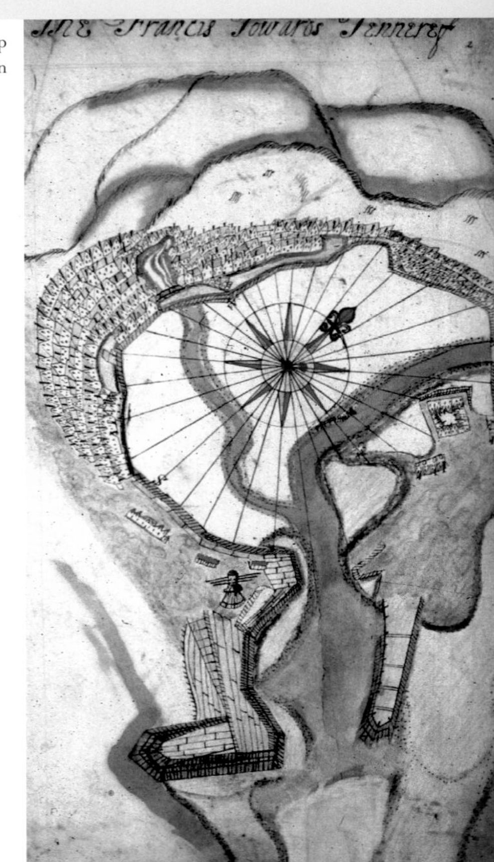

1684 harbour map shows an inner basin

## Creation of an inner basin

An appeal to the Crown in 1660 about the poor state of the harbour and the threat of ruin for hundreds of local families was successful and the Passing Tolls Act was renewed in 1662 for eight years, but not enough money was raised to do what was really necessary. Some improvements were made, however. In 1661 Thomas Digges' Great Paradise was cut in half by a crosswall of chalk, forming an inner basin – the forerunner of the Granville Dock. Gates enabled ships to pass from the tidal harbour, but only at high tide and when water was needed for scouring ships in the inner basin, ships were left high and dry! At the same time new gates opposite the harbour mouth provided a much greater flow of water when open to clear shingle from the harbour mouth. Strond Street and later Custom House Quay were built on the silted up canal to Little Paradise. From 1670 onwards quays and warehouses were built there.

King Louis XIV

# The Secret Treaty of Dover

In 1670 Charles II's sister, Minette, came over from France and was met by Charles. They stayed at Dover Castle for about a fortnight during which the infamous Secret Treaty of Dover was signed. Louis XIV of France, the 'Sun King', wanted England to return to Catholicism. Parliament and the country at large hated Catholics, but Louis thought Charles would swear to anything if it was financially advantageous – he might even declare himself Catholic for a price! Charles was officially Anglican, but privately Catholic. After all, Charles' wife, brother, brother's wife, favourite sister and favourite mistress were all Catholic. Charles negotiated secretly with Louis. Minette, Duchess of Orleans, Charles' youngest sister and Louis' sister-in-law, was used as the go-between. She was anxious to see France and England united as rulers of the world and her brother publicly converted to Catholicism. Charles demanded £200,000 to declare himself Catholic, more cash if rebellion broke out and £600,000 for English help against the Dutch, plus Ostend, Minorca and the Spanish American possessions. According to Louis these demands 'were a thunderclap that took his breath away'. Charles put pressure on by persuading Parliament to put an import duty on wine and vinegar. A compromise was reached and the secret treaty was brought to Dover for signature under cover of a state visit by Minette. It was concealed from the public and would have meant civil war if revealed. The key point was an undertaking by Charles to declare himself Catholic at a time of his own choosing, thereby reconciling England with Rome. Louis promised £140,000 and 6,000 soldiers to help Charles suppress any subsequent English rebellion. Both agreed to declare war on Holland for which Charles was to be paid £200,000 for each year of war with the Dutch, but only after Charles had declared himself Catholic. Minette was certain she had scored a diplomatic triumph after months of intrigue. Fireworks celebrated the event – but nobody knew why! On leaving Dover, Minette offered Charles a jewel from her jewel box. He replied, 'The only jewel I covet is Louise,' – a 19 year old maid of honour to Minette! Charles' beloved sister returned to France, where she died eight days later aged 26. Louise did later become another of Charles' mistresses.

Duke of York who became James II

## James II

On 21 June 1672 Princess Mary of Modena, aged 15, landed at Dover and was met by the King's brother, James, Duke of York, who had been Lord Warden from 1660 to 1669. The princess was married to him later the same evening before they left Dover. Children by the Duke's first wife had been brought up as protestants, but he had converted to Catholicism and his second wife was also Catholic. This prompted parliament to try to exclude James from the throne.

Despite this, James did succeed his brother in 1685; however, his attempts to restore England to Catholicism were strongly opposed and the birth of a male heir, who would also be Catholic, triggered his downfall in 1688 when parliament invited protestants William of Orange and his wife Mary – James' daughter – to replace him. On 3 November of that year the Prince of Orange anchored off Dover with an army and a fleet of more than 500 ships, but unfavourable weather prevented him from landing. He sailed westward and landed at Torbay in Devon to claim the throne.

## Harbour in a sorry state

In the meantime Dover Harbour was in a sorry state with the beach barrier preventing ships sailing in or out of the harbour. The resultant lack of commerce caused businesses to fail and unemployment to rise. In 1682 Charles II called for a report on how to improve matters at a harbour so important to England. Nothing came of it. In 1697 William III ordered the Lords of the Admiralty to remedy the situation. Admiral Sir Cloudesley Shovel recommended a better crosswall, new sluices and the rebuilding of the piers at a cost of £8,000. This was too expensive for Dover and with no help from the King, the report was shelved. By 1699 only small boats could enter the harbour at all states of the tide. The cross-Channel

Harbour in 1738

packet boats could only enter at the high spring tides; otherwise, they had to wait outside for a boat to arrive and tell them whether it was safe to enter. If there was less than six feet of water they anchored outside and both mail and passengers were taken ashore by small boat. Needless to say this was time consuming and expensive. Sir Henry Shears asked parliament for £30,000 to improve matters. Instead the Passing Tolls Act was renewed for nine years, which was subsequently extended again and again until finally abolished in 1861. This provided just enough money for Sir Cloudesley Shovel's recommendations to be carried out.

## Lovesick Henry Matson

In 1720 the Harbour Commissioners had a welcome windfall when Henry Matson died and left all his estates to Dover Harbour. However, there was a condition. Once a year the wooden decking of the harbour's piers were to be inspected for any holes caused by missing wooden pegs, called pegs-a-trunnel. These were to be plugged immediately to prevent gentlemen's walking sticks from falling through. This strange requirement stemmed from a sad tale of unrequited love. Henry, a local landowner, had set his heart on marrying Elizabeth Stokes, daughter of master mariner and six times mayor, William Stokes. Whilst taking his usual walk along one of the piers, his gold topped cane slipped through a hole in the decking where a peg should have been and was lost to the sea. Churchwarden Henry forgot himself and swore out loud. Unfortunately for him, Elizabeth and her mother were in earshot and that was the end of their friendship. Elizabeth married another, but lovesick Henry never married. The Commissioners carried out his wishes for years, but eventually the duty was forgotten; however, the annual Trunnel Feast, always held after the inspection at the expense of the Matson estate, survived much longer! Eventually Matson's lands were sold off and the income was used to improve the harbour.

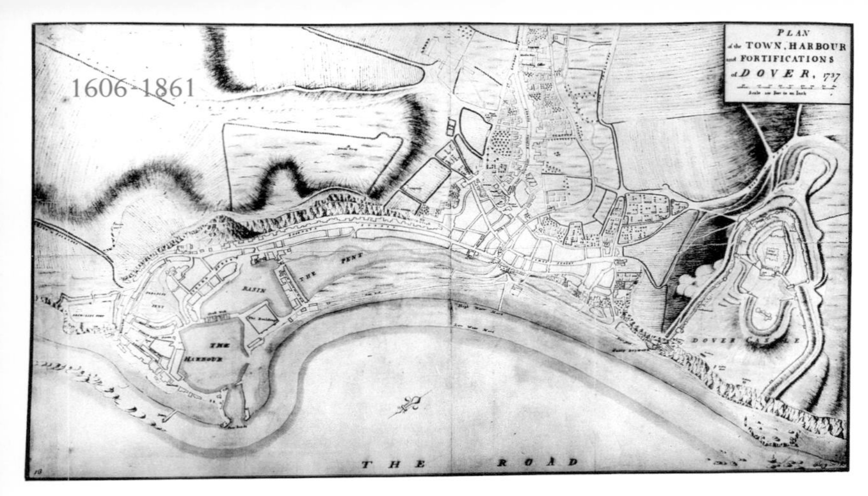


1737 plan of the harbour

# Various improvement plans

During the 18th and early 19th centuries various plans were submitted for the improvement of the harbour. They all recognised the need for a long pier of some sort sufficiently far into deep water to keep the shingle away; however, it was not technically possible at that time and was beyond local resources. The ideas also greatly underestimated the length of pier required – 200 feet was the longest mentioned compared with the original Admiralty Pier that was built between 1847 and 1871 of 2100 feet which was itself extended another 2000 feet at the end of the century!

The North and South Piers were repaired in 1718 and a small jetty built south-west of the harbour mouth called Cheeseman's Head. James Hammond, son of the owner of Hammond's Quay, was Clerk of Dover Harbour when in 1729 he called for much needed repairs. He was the driving force for the many improvements that followed. In 1727 a gate was inserted between the Pent and the inner basin, allowing small ships into the Pent – the forerunner of the Wellington Dock. To help protect the sea wall of the Pent Castle Jetty was built in 1752 to encourage the build-up of a shingle bank in front of the Pent sea wall. Such was the build-up that houses were built on it from 1816. It was still difficult to get into Dover Harbour! In the second half of the 18th century three major reports were submitted with ambitious plans, but Dover Harbour Board was not impressed and only carried out minor improvements. One plan proposed a brand new harbour inland near the Maison Dieu, requiring the dredging of the River Dour to make it navigable

Castle Jetty, built 1752

George I



## House of Hanover

When Queen Anne died in1714, the Stuart era ended and George I, Elector of Hanover became the first Hanoverian king. He was frequently in Hanover. Returning to Britain in 1726, he sailed from Holland and entered Dover harbour, but due to bad weather he could not land and eventually landed at Rye! George III began his long reign in 1760 and his pig-headedness is often blamed for Britain losing its American colonies. At the beginning of the 19th century, George III visited the Kent coast to inspect the arrangements against the threat of an invasion by Napoleon and encouraged the raising of a large army of Cinque Ports' Volunteers under William Pitt, his Prime Minister, who was also Lord Warden.

Queen Anne

## Yet more harbour plans but little action

There were plans to allow more and larger ships into the harbour, but they were not adopted. Still bedevilled by a shingle bar, larger ships could only enter at high tide. A flag was raised from the pier head when water at the mouth reached a depth of ten feet and was lowered when it fell below. Owing to the Napoleonic threat there was no organised cross-Channel traffic at this time, although previously there had been 30 sailing ships working the Passage plus five mail packets which could reach Calais in three hours in favourable conditions, but could take up to 24 hours!

The Harbour Board sought professional advice, asking civil engineers, Rennie and Walker, to suggest improvements. Their report in 1802 recommended lengthening the South Pier by 270 feet as far as low water mark, curved at the end to deflect shingle past the mouth, improvements to the sluices, deepening the Pent and basin, building a dry dock and the widening of the lock and gates between the tidal harbour and basin. Once again the proposals were ignored, bearing in mind the estimated cost was £54,000! With the town of Dover highly dependent upon an accessible harbour for trade and travellers, relations with the Harbour Board were strained to the limit.

North and South pierheads

The allied sovereigns of the Napoleonic Wars at a review in the 1820s
From the left:
the Duke of Wellington,
King of Prussia, George IV
and the Emperor of Russia

## Restoration of the French monarchy

Czar of Russia and the King of Prussia landing by Archcliffe Fort

The town of Dover was packed with people on 23rd April 1814 and some had walked 40 miles. This was to see the arrival of the Duke of Clarence at Dover with his brother, the Prince Regent, accompanying Louis XVIII to Dover on his way to reclaim the French throne, following the abdication of Napoleon Bonaparte. The streets were lined with troops and after sleeping overnight in Dover – the Prince Regent at Mr Fector's house and Louis on board the royal yacht – Louis sailed away to great crowds of onlookers, salutes from the coastal batteries and warships decorated with the flags of both nations.

Soon afterwards, on 6 June 1814, *HMS Impregnable*, commanded by the same Duke of Clarence, arrived at Dover from Boulogne, carrying Czar Alexander I of Russia and the King of Prussia. They had come to Britain to join in the premature celebrations of the defeat of Napoleon. Owing to the state of tide, they landed on a platform in front of Archcliffe Fort and stayed in Dover overnight – Alexander with Mr Fector, the banker, the King of Prussia at the York Hotel and Marshal Blücher at the Ship Inn. They returned to the continent on 26 June.

## Royal Dukes

At least two royal dukes were in Dover in 1818. On 25 May the Duke of Cumberland arrived on the royal yacht with his bride and on 6 September the Duke and Duchess of Kent, parents of Victoria who later became queen, left for the continent and returned the following year.

Caroline of Brunswick
Queen of George IV

## George IV and Queen Caroline

George III died in 1820 and his son, the Prince Regent, who had undertaken the monarch's duties for some years due to his father's 'madness,' became George IV. This prompted Queen Caroline, the estranged wife of George IV, to land in Dover on 5 June on her way to London to assert her position as Queen of England. A large crowd greeted her on the beach and she took refuge in the York Hotel. Apparently there was some confusion during her stay in Dover because, as the estranged wife of the King, her status was not clear. The local army commander fired guns in salute and provided mounted guards of honour, but the Mayor and Corporation did not appear for the traditional welcome for a monarch. She died a year later aged 53. This unfortunate lady had been married to George since 1795 and, because of his dislike for her, had won public sympathy, running an orphanage at Blackheath for many years.

The Prince Regent,
later George IV

## Arrival of steam

*Rob Roy* was the first steamship to enter Dover harbour on 10 June 1821 and soon crossed the Channel for the first time. Only a few passengers were brave enough to try the new-fangled contraption, but the sceptics were quickly won over. The age of steam had arrived.

The first steam packet, the *Rob Roy*, arriving at Dover

Dover Pier and Castle, taken from Cheeseman's Jetty in 1809

## Oxenden and Moon's harbour improvements

Minor improvements to the harbour were made at a leisurely pace from the end of the 18th century for the next thirty years by two enthusiastic men: James Moon, harbour master and the first resident engineer from 1792 to 1832 and Sir Henry Oxenden, a local gentleman living at Broome Park, who was appointed to the Harbour Board at the age of 28 and took charge of the harbour works from 1791. Sir Henry provided a new swingbridge for the lower crosswall made by carpenters at Broome Park and transported complete to Dover! The talented Oxenden also built a horseless carriage that used wind power, reaching 32 mph! The North and South Piers were repaired following the great storm of 1808. A new wet dock and a new dry dock were built; by 1821 a new crosswall and basin were built. Gas lights replaced candles at the pier heads in 1823. New stone quays were provided in various parts of the basin, replacing the old timber and brick. In 1823 the outer harbour was deepened by four feet by the removal of 18,000 tons of mud and by 1827 both the North and South Piers had been rebuilt. In 1830 work began on Moon's plans for the Pent, which involved removing mud to provide more water and lining the whole Pent with a continuous stone quay plus new lock gates. The work was finished by 1832. The wet and dry docks in the outer harbour had robbed it of a good deal of water, leaving only room for a few ships to enter and shelter. The shingle was still a menace and the sluices often disappointed, but they were improved in 1834 by James Walker, who had taken over from James Moon following his death. Sir Henry Oxenden supervised. The Duke of Wellington, hero of Waterloo and prime minister, had been appointed Lord Warden in 1829 and gave powerful support to Oxenden, but Wellington could only use the finance and engineering expertise available.

Town and harbour in the 1830s

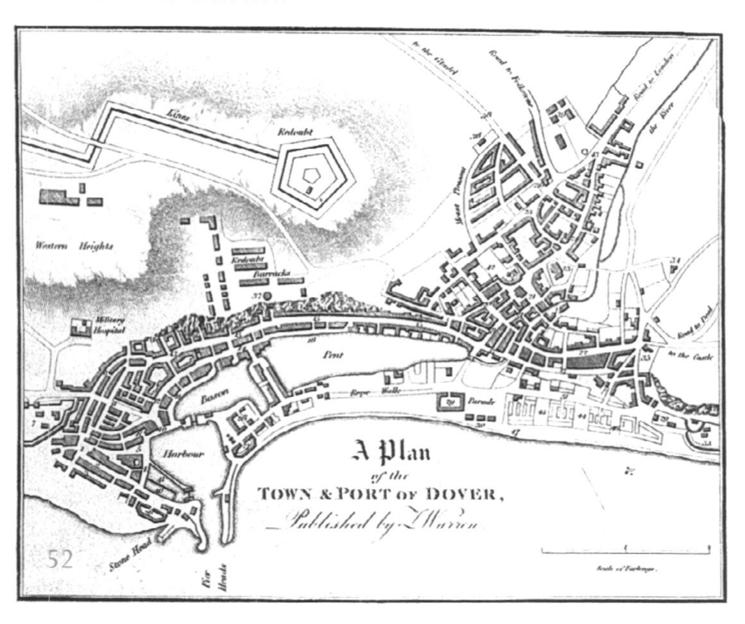

Pierhead in 1834

## Harbour Board criticised

Criticism of the Harbour Board became more and more vocal. None of the work had tackled the root problem of keeping the harbour clear of shingle. Every ship diverted was a loss to local tradesmen. Townsfolk held a public meeting in the Paris Hotel on New Year's Day 1834 where the Harbour Board was criticised for squandering its income on grandiose schemes that were doomed to failure. An appeal was made to the Harbour Board and the government to implement all the recommendations, dating from Henry VIII's time, for a long projection out to sea. The Lord Warden called in the famous civil engineer, Telford, whose recommendations for improvements to the sluices, tunnels and culverts were completed by 1838. At this time the board, which usually met twice a year, comprised three ex-officio members: the Lord Warden, the Lieutenant Governor of Dover Castle and the Mayor of Dover plus Sir Henry Oxenden of Broome Park (who lived 7 miles away) W. O. Hammond of St Albans (8 miles), Sir Edward Knatchbull of Mersham Hatch (19 miles), Sir John Bridges of Wootton Court (8 miles), J P Plumptre of Fredville Park (8 miles), The Earl of Guilford of Waldershare Park (6 miles), Sir B. Bridges of Goodnestone Park (9 miles) and F. Morrice of Betteshanger (8 miles). Henshaw Latham was treasurer, like his father and grandfather before him. John Shipdem was the register, auditor, conveyancer, solicitor and agent for the Dover Harbour tonnage dues. Other employees were the receiver of wharfage and crane dues, receiver of harbour rent, who was also the architect cum surveyor, clerk of the cheque, who checked the times of arrival and departure of workmen and accounted for all materials, the harbour master and his deputy, foreman of carpenters, two foremen of labourers, regulator of the harbour clock, bridge shifter, messenger and bell ringer.

Thomas Telford, Engineer

Quay scene in 1840

## The 1836 inquiry

In 1836 a crisis was reached when the Harbour Board promoted a parliamentary bill for more powers. Instead, the bill was blocked and the Board was subjected to a searching public enquiry. The committee of inquiry comprised 15 MPs, five of whom were from Kent and included two, Knatchbull and Plumptre, who were members of the Harbour Board. They only took seven days. Since 1828 Passing Tolls had been granted indefinitely and now yielded some six to seven thousand pounds a year in total from every port in Britain and Ireland. Rents from harbour properties raised £2,500 a year, wharfage dues £800 a year. There was £1443 in the bank but liabilities totalled £64,000. A loan of £60,000 was needed. The 20 witnesses, both local and experts appointed by the government, gave conflicting evidence. In the subsequent report to the House of Commons the committee came to no conclusions about the harbour itself, but recommended changes to its management. Works already started were to be completed but in future plans should be submitted for approval to the Admiralty. All estimates and accounts were to be laid annually before Parliament. In the Commons a resolution that all the powers of the Board should be transferred to the Lords of the Admiralty failed, but only on a technicality. These changes required an act of parliament, which did not materialise until 1861.

The landing of
Prince Albert at Dover

# The arrival of Prince Albert

An important occasion for Dover and the whole country was 6 February 1840 when Prince Albert of Saxe Coburg arrived at Dover, after a rough crossing, on his way to marry Victoria, who had become queen in 1837 following the death of her uncle William IV. The cross-Channel packet ship *Ariel*, accompanied by *HMS Firebrand*, arrived. On entering the harbour the cutters *Vigilant* and *Victoria* saluted them and loud cheering could be heard from crowds on the North and South Pier heads and quays. Albert was received by the commander of the garrison with a guard of honour and was then escorted to the York Hotel. The mayor and other dignitaries were in attendance. A royal salute was fired from the Western Heights above as the prince appeared at a hotel window to more cheering. Next morning, two troops of Dragoons arrived from Canterbury commanded by the Earl of Cardigan and were drawn up in front of the York Hotel. The mayor, recorder, aldermen and other corporation members in their robes, attended by the mace-bearer, arrived with an address of congratulation. The prince replied and then left Dover and its cheering crowds in seven carriages, escorted by the troops and with a deafening royal salute fired from the shore batteries.

On 14 November 1842 Victoria and Albert drove to Dover from Walmer Castle, the official residence of the Lord Warden, where they were staying with the Duke of Wellington – hero of Waterloo, former prime minister and Lord Warden of the Cinque Ports. Despite short notice the town was quickly decorated and crowds turned out. After visiting Dover Castle and enjoying the Channel views, they went into the town via the newly laid out Castle Street. A royal salute was fired during the tour. Victoria would have passed the Ship Hotel where she stayed as a child with her mother, the Duchess of Kent. The Prince Consort was in Dover once again on 28 March 1844 when he visited Archcliffe Fort and then left for the Continent, returning on 11 April.

Prince Albert leaving
Dover for London, 1840

Dover Town Station
from Shakespeare Cliff

## Coming of the railway

As early as 1820 there were 12 stage coaches daily to London from various Dover inns and hotels. The mail coach journey took nine hours. All this activity was to change with the coming of the railway. In order to cover only six miles to Dover from Folkestone the London and South Eastern Railway Company had to build the mighty Foord Viaduct in Folkestone, two major tunnels, demolish 300 feet of chalk cliff, construct a timber viaduct across Shakespeare Beach and build a terminus close to the shore at Archcliffe called Town Station. When the line opened on 7 February 1844 6,000 people lined the rails and 300 guests attended a banquet at a Snargate Street theatre. Ladies were allowed to attend as a special privilege, but were obliged to sit in the gallery and watch only! The impressive Lord Warden Hotel adjoining the Town Station was built in 1851. The London, Chatham and Dover railway line did not reach Dover until 1861, terminating initially at Priory Station, but then extended through the cliff to the new Harbour Station in the Pier District. This gave the harbour two different lines to London. With the coming of the railway linking Dover to London, many more cross-Channel journeys were undertaken and this included members of the royal family.

A Dover stagecoach in 1841

Painting by William Burgess 'Working on the new Wellington Dock, 1842'

The Harbour, about 1850

## Wellington Dock and other improvements

Between 1840 and 1843 improvements to the Pent were made with all the quays rebuilt with stone and then work started on enlarging the tidal harbour by removing a large area of land in the north-east corner. This enabled construction of a new entrance from the tidal harbour into the Pent through an opening in Union Street with lock gates for shipping and a bridge for the public. This was a large undertaking, involving the demolition of the old Amherst Battery and many Union Street buildings plus the removal of 3,000 wagon loads of soil a week from 1844 to 1846. To open the new bridge named after him the Duke of Wellington, the most active Lord Warden and Chairman of the Harbour Board, drove over it in his carriage with 19 guns thundering from the Western Heights. Other improvements followed in quick succession. The harbour mouth was deepened to low water mark, a slipway was provided in the Wellington Dock for ship repairs, the River Dour was roofed over for 330 feet downstream from New Bridge, later becoming Cambridge Terrace and land was reclaimed from Wellington Dock to form Northampton Street. Shipyards displaced from Shakespeare Beach by the railway construction moved to Cambridge Road, flanking the Wellington Dock. Due to the demand for faster and larger vessels, this old local industry had declined from 40 or so shipwrights in the early 19th century to a mere handful.

Engraving of Wellington Bridge, 1846

Stanfield painting of the building of the Admiralty Pier

Last official visit by Wellington in 1850 to see Admiralty Pier progress

# Need for a national harbour of refuge

From 1840 the Admiralty was concerned about the lack of any harbour round the south coast from the Thames estuary in the east to Selsey Bill in the west that could shelter any class of vessel under all wind and tide conditions. There was also no existing harbour that could be improved to make it accessible at low water. An inquiry suggested a harbour at Dover enclosing 450 acres of the bay by building two piers from the shore with a breakwater 1000 yards from shore. The Admiralty dithered over what to do. Variations on the original suggestion were considered and yet another inquiry was set up and once again, in 1846, Dover was recommended for the much needed strategic harbour. Finally, in 1847 the Admiralty decided to construct only the west pier and early in 1851, long before the whole length was completed, cross-Channel steamers were able to berth alongside at any state of the tide. Before the pier, known as Admiralty Pier, was finished, both railway companies extended their lines on to the pier to enable mail and passengers to transfer easily from train to ship. In 1860 a line was laid and opened from the Town Station, which went straight through the basement of the rebuilt Pilot House on to the pier and in 1864 the line from Harbour Station on to the pier was completed. Quite by chance the London, Chatham and Dover company made a publicity coup when a royal train used the line on its first day when Queen Victoria's son, the Duke of Cambridge, and Princess Mary arrived to go to France – it was claimed that the line had been opened by royalty!

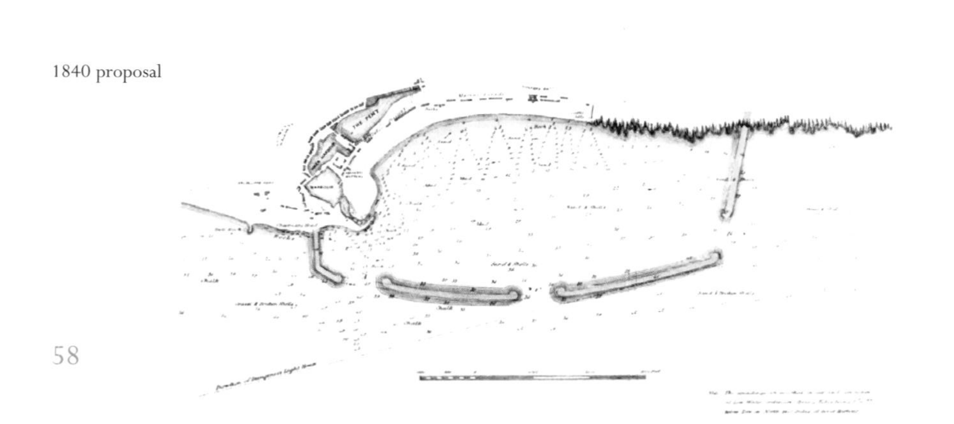

1840 proposal

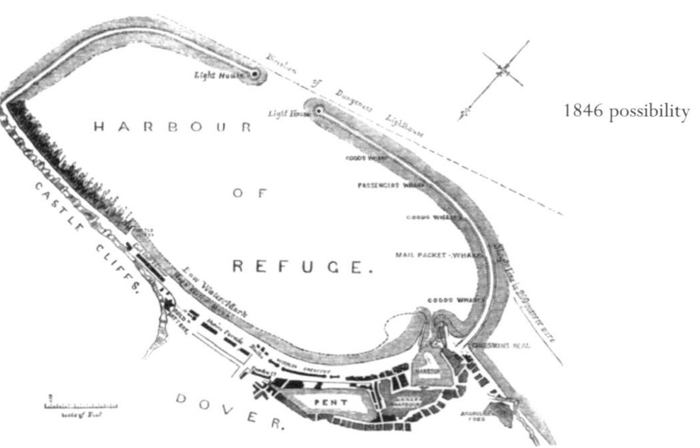


1846 possibility

Royal Yacht *Victoria and Albert* in Dover Bay, 1850

## Surprise visit

Queen Victoria made an unscheduled, surprise visit to the harbour on 23 August 1850 as she was returning to the Isle of Wight. A cross-Channel mailboat spotted the royal squadron in the Channel and gave Dover some advance warning. By the time the royal yacht *Victoria and Albert* was sighted, the cliffs above the town and the sea front were packed with people. The yacht anchored near the old harbour's mouth with its royal standard flying, matched by others on the Western Heights and Dover Castle. All the boats in harbour had hastily dressed overall. A salute from the castle followed by a 21 gun salute from the Artillery Battery shook the houses below. Prince Albert went on deck, acknowledging the cheers from ship and shore by bowing repeatedly. Apparently Victoria spent her time sketching, but did appear on the bridge of the paddleboat. Nobody knew whether she intended to come ashore so preparations were made in case she landed. The couple retired below for dinner at 8pm, however, and then the royal squadron weighed anchor and the crowds dispersed during a final royal salute.

## Shingle problem solved at long last

The Admiralty Pier became, in effect a narrow railway station with three landing jetties on the inner side and two on the outer. When the 1800 foot pier was completed in 1864 there were complaints in parliament that it still did not meet the Royal Navy's need for a harbour of refuge, but it did solve the long standing shingle problem of the old harbour! The pier had no proper end to it, but there was a need to deflect the tidal current by extending the pier still further in order to protect the rest of the pier from being undermined. With conflicting ideas about how to achieve this, the Board of Trade, to whom the pier had been transferred by the Admiralty, started in 1867 to extend the pier by 300 feet in a curved direction.

Arrival of Napoleon III in 1855

# Louis Napoleon

All this building activity in Dover Harbour did not stop the comings and goings of important people across the Channel. Louis Napoleon was the nephew of Napoleon Bonaparte. Louis first arrived with his mother, Bonaparte's sister, in Dover in 1831 after having to leave France in disguise. After a year or so he left England but returned again in 1838 to prepare an 'invasion' of France. This hopeless attempt was made in 1840 when he was arrested in Boulogne without a shot being fired and imprisoned. He escaped in 1845 and once again returned to England. His fortune changed in 1848 when he was elected president of the new republic, following the overthrow of King Louis Philippe. Within three years he made himself Emperor of France. Queen Victoria and Prince Albert visited him in Paris in 1855. Dover was the scene for a grand occasion on 16 April 1855 when Prince Albert met Napoleon III, as he called himself, when he landed at Dover on his way to visit Queen Victoria for a six day State visit. The whole town was excited. Guards of honour lined the way and cannons thundered from all quarters as they walked to the Lord Warden Hotel with the Empress Eugenie on the arm of Prince Albert.

Tragedy overtook the French Emperor in 1870 when his army surrendered to the Prussian army and France was declared a republic. The Emperor's family fled to England. The Prince Imperial arrived in Dover on 6 September and on the following day Empress Eugenie landed secretly on the Isle of Wight. After spending some time as the prisoner of the Prussians, Louis Napoleon landed yet again at Dover on 20 March 1871 as a refugee once more. A large crowd awaited his arrival on the Comte de Flanders on Admiralty Pier, but things went badly wrong. Apparently the wrong flag was hoisted, resulting in the ship berthing in the old harbour at Crosswall Quay, where there was nobody to greet him. Looking remarkably well despite reports of ill health, he was soon reunited with his wife and son. After a brief visit to the Lord Warden Hotel they set off by train for Chislehurst, where Napoleon III's exile only lasted two years before he died.

Reception of Napoleon III and Empress Eugenie at The Lord Warden Hotel

## Queen Victoria arrives unexpectedly again

Dover had only 24 hours notice of the possible arrival of Queen Victoria and Prince Albert on 31 August 1858. They were returning from a visit to Berlin and were expected to land at Gravesend where the Mayor and Corporation and the state railway carriages awaited them, but after leaving Antwerp Victoria gave orders for the royal yacht *Victoria and Albert* to steam to Dover. Fortunately, Lord Malmesbury had landed at Dover the day before and had warned that the royal couple might arrive. The local naval and military commanders quickly made contingency arrangements to welcome the Queen. The royal yacht duly appeared, accompanied only by the Trinity House yacht *Irene* – the squadron of naval escort vessels had steamed to Gravesend as ordered! The customary 21 gun royal salute was fired and then a boat was sent to find out what the Queen wished to do. She wanted to land. The royal yacht berthed at the Admiralty Pier, Victoria and Albert disembarked and inspected the guards of honour whilst a special train was prepared for them. Dr Astley, Mayor of Dover, was present, but with such short notice there was no customary official welcome by the corporation. The royal party soon left with crowds cheering the train on its way.

Sadly, Prince Albert died of typhoid, aged 42 in 1861. The country had been very suspicious of this German prince when he first came to England, but Albert earned tremendous respect by the model he and Queen Victoria set for family life as well as by his hard work, including his greatest triumph, the Great Exhibition of 1851 held at the specially built Crystal Palace in Hyde Park.

Queen Victoria

# Chapter 3 1861-1945

At the end f the First World War, Field Marshal Haig
was welcomed by the wartime mayor, Sir Edwin Farley.
Haig replied to the Mayor's address.

*'The oldest of the Cinque Ports has worthily sustained its reputation and the days of the Dover Patrol constitute a record of which Dover, with all its historical associations, may well be proud.'*

Admiralty Pier about 1875 with the Lord Warden Hotel and Town Station

## Changes to the Harbour Board

In 1861, some 25 years after the report to parliament had called for changes in the constitution of the Harbour Board, the government proposed that from 1 January 1862 the Passing Tolls Act, which had provided some income for the harbour for hundreds of years and was still worth £10,000 a year, should be abolished and that management of the harbour should be transferred from the Warden and Assistants to a Board of Trustees to be called the Dover Harbour Board. Alarmed at the prospect of losing their sinecure, the sitting tenants appealed to Prime Minister Palmerston, who turned the tables on them and persuaded them to resign! The first meeting of the reconstituted Harbour Board met on 1 September 1861 with Lord Palmerston himself as Chairman, being Lord Warden of the Cinque Ports. As urged by Dover Corporation the other six members were nominees from the Admiralty, the Board of Trade, from each railway company and two from Dover Corporation.

Test firing at the Gun Turret, 1885

## Granville Dock and arming of Admiralty Pier

With little money and substantial debts to repay, no major works were attempted by the new board for some years. Rebuilding of the inner basin was completed in 1874 and was named Granville Dock after Earl Granville, Lord Warden and Chairman of the Board.

Changes were made to the Admiralty Pier, however. In 1871 work began on building a fort at its extremity. The main structure was not finished until 1880 and then its armoured turret was added a year later, but it was not finally equipped and ready until 1885. Armament comprised two 81 ton guns mounted in a revolving turret. The guns were test fired in 1885 and, much to the surprise of many, Admiralty Pier did not collapse from the vibration!

Despite the new pier and the improvements made to the old harbour since 1840, cross-Channel facilities were still not good enough. A deep harbour at Dover able to accommodate larger ships was of little use if those ships could not enter the harbours at Calais or Boulogne.

Custom House Quay
in the 1870s

## Arrivals of the Queen of Denmark

Once Victoria's eldest son, known as Bertie within the family, came of age, he was a frequent visitor to Dover Harbour for the rest of his life both as Prince of Wales and later as Edward VII. He would be en route for the continent, visiting India and other parts of the empire or making official visits to the harbour. In addition it often fell to him, before he became King, to come to Dover to welcome foreign heads of state on behalf of his mother. So it was on 12 October 1866 when the Prince of Wales arrived by train with the Danish Ambassador to welcome the Queen of Denmark and her two children who had travelled on the *Vivid* from Calais. After berthing at the Admiralty Pier, they took a late lunch at the Lord Warden Hotel before boarding the special train for London.

The Queen of Denmark landed again on 2 November 1875 with her husband the King and their daughter, Princess Thyra. This time they were welcomed by Alexandra, Princess of Wales, who was Danish herself, and by the royal Dukes of Edinburgh and Cambridge.
As always on these occasions the Admiralty Pier was crowded with onlookers as the royal party, showing no ill effects from the rough crossing, disembarked; the royal salute was fired and the guard of honour from the 78th Highlanders was inspected. The royal party then boarded the special train drawn up on the pier as the Danish national anthem was played amidst the cheers of the crowd.

Prince of Wales, with his bride, Princess Alexandra, at Sandringham in 1863, the year of their wedding

Landing of the Duke and Duchess of Cambridge at Dover

# Arrival of the Sultan of Turkey

During July 1867 the Duke of Cambridge and Prince Teck arrived from Calais on the mail steam packet *Samphire*, having attended the International exhibition in Paris. After some refreshment at the Lord Warden Hotel they boarded a train for London. In the same month on 12 July, the Prince of Wales and his brother, the Duke of Cambridge, came to Dover and, after staying in the Lord Warden Hotel overnight, welcomed the Sultan of Turkey at the Admiralty Pier in the French Imperial yacht *Reine Hortense*, accompanied by French naval vessels. A gun was fired from the Calais fort to signal the Sultan's departure from Boulogne and the welcoming party then made its way to the Admiralty Pier. Other dignitaries had arrived by special train during the morning. The royal brothers, dressed in Field Marshal uniforms, went on board to meet the Sultan. As they came ashore salutes resounded from all the forts and batteries and from ships of the British and French navies dressed overall. State carriages took them along the pier, which was covered in scarlet cloth, to the Lord Warden Hotel where troops and four military bands awaited them in the forecourt. Inside the hotel the Sultan breakfasted with his family in one room, the Prince of Wales and his companions in another and the rest of the party ate in the main dining room. Following an address of welcome by the Mayor and Corporation, a special train comprising four state saloon carriages, twelve first class carriages and luggage vans took them to London.

Arrival of the Sultan of Turkey

Entrance to Granville Dock in the 1870s

## The Shah of Persia

Another grand occasion for Dover and its harbour was on 18 June 1873 when the Shah of Persia arrived from Ostend to visit Britain. Vast crowds, not only from Dover, awaited his arrival with no soldiers or police in evidence. Vessels of all descriptions thronged the harbour. A royal salute fired from the castle heralded the arrival of the train carrying the Duke of Edinburgh and Prince Arthur of Connaught who were to welcome the Shah on behalf of Queen Victoria. The *Enchantress*, carrying the Lords of the Admiralty, steamed out of the harbour to join eight warships escorting the Shah in the royal yacht *Vigilant*. Firing of heavy guns out to sea announced the arrival of the royal squadron. The large welcoming party, comprising notables both local and national including the Mayor and Corporation and the Lord Warden, Earl Granville, went on board to greet the royal visitor. A band played a Persian march as the Shah disembarked, wearing a coat faced with rows of diamonds and rubies. As he walked along the red carpet acknowledging the cheers of the crowd, the diamond encrusted scabbard of his scimitar sparkled in the sun. The Shah retired to a specially prepared room in the Lord Warden Hotel for a few minutes and then emerged to hear the address of welcome from the mayor. Since the Shah spoke no English, it was then interpreted and then the Shah replied, saying that he felt among friends. That also had to be interpreted. During a leisurely lunch in the hotel the band of the 3rd Buffs played outside the windows and then the royal train departed for London from the brightly decorated station. Apparently he was not impressed with the speed of the train and on arrival in London demanded that the driver be executed for travelling too fast! The Shah brought with him his favourite hunting hound called *Ootchac*, but apparently he was not allowed to own a dog because for Moslems it was an impure animal; therefore, it was owned officially by one of his party who, presumably, was not a Moslem!

Shah of Persia accompanied by the Dukes of Edinburgh and Connaught

The Czar arriving at Dover, 1874

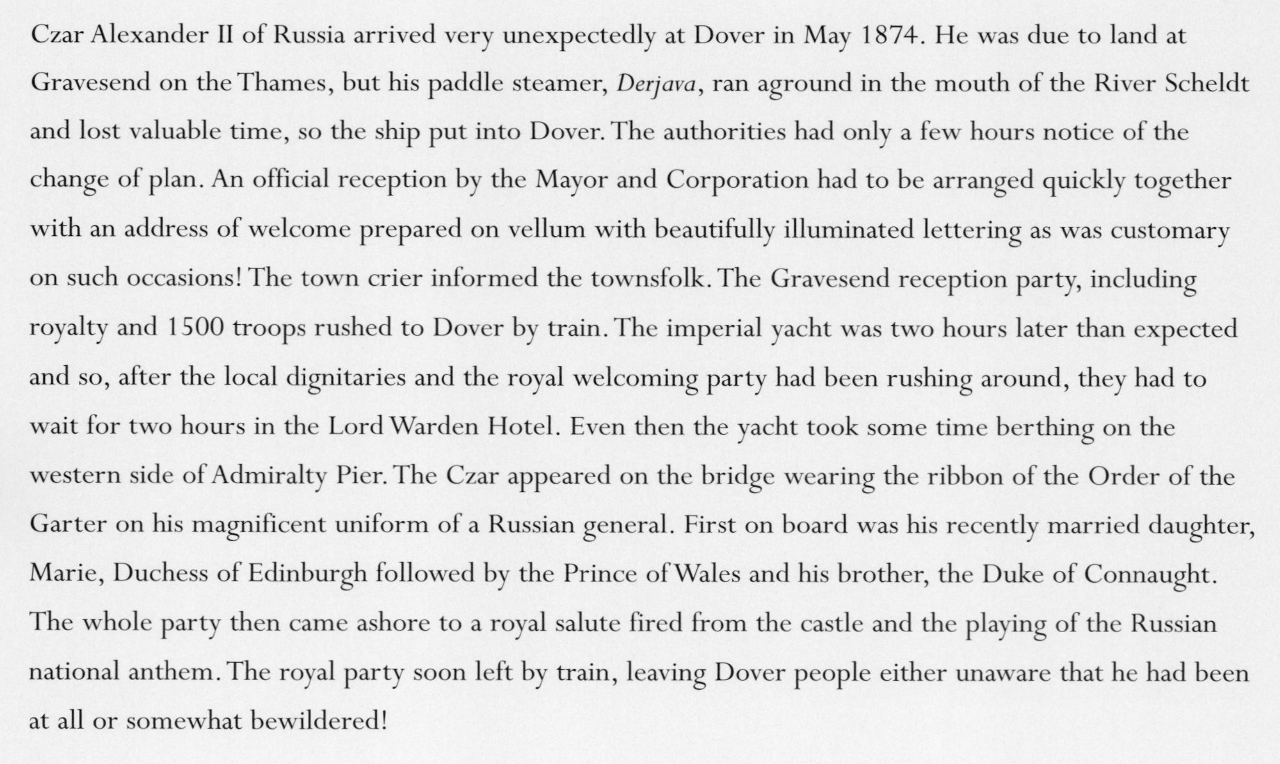

# The Czar of Russia

Czar Alexander II of Russia arrived very unexpectedly at Dover in May 1874. He was due to land at Gravesend on the Thames, but his paddle steamer, *Derjava*, ran aground in the mouth of the River Scheldt and lost valuable time, so the ship put into Dover. The authorities had only a few hours notice of the change of plan. An official reception by the Mayor and Corporation had to be arranged quickly together with an address of welcome prepared on vellum with beautifully illuminated lettering as was customary on such occasions! The town crier informed the townsfolk. The Gravesend reception party, including royalty and 1500 troops rushed to Dover by train. The imperial yacht was two hours later than expected and so, after the local dignitaries and the royal welcoming party had been rushing around, they had to wait for two hours in the Lord Warden Hotel. Even then the yacht took some time berthing on the western side of Admiralty Pier. The Czar appeared on the bridge wearing the ribbon of the Order of the Garter on his magnificent uniform of a Russian general. First on board was his recently married daughter, Marie, Duchess of Edinburgh followed by the Prince of Wales and his brother, the Duke of Connaught. The whole party then came ashore to a royal salute fired from the castle and the playing of the Russian national anthem. The royal party soon left by train, leaving Dover people either unaware that he had been at all or somewhat bewildered!

Alexander II

The ill-fated *Castilia*

## Prince of Wales and the Castilia

In 1875 the Prince of Wales travelled from Dover to Calais on his way to India in the *Castilia*, which was one of a number of peculiar vessels that were tried on the cross-Channel routes around this time. The *Castilia* was designed by Captain Dicey, a former captain in the Indian Navy, and named after Lady Granville, wife of the Harbour Board Chairman and Lord Warden. Launched in 1874, it was the largest cross-Channel vessel so far built, comprising two half hulls connected by cross girders with a waterway between in which the paddles operated. Both ends of the vessel were identical each with a rudder, making turning unnecessary. It was much slower than conventional ships on the route, however, and after a few years was taken out of service to become a floating hospital for infectious diseases!

## King of Hanover

Representatives of the British royal family did not always welcome foreign royals at Dover. With the advent of the railways, the royal welcome was sometimes performed at the London station of arrival. Such an occasion was the arrival of the King of Hanover in 1876. This grandson of George III and Victoria's cousin was welcomed in London by the Prince and Princess of Wales with very little ceremony at Dover. When the blind king arrived at Dover again on 23 June 1878, it was even more low key. There was no welcoming party at all at Dover for the dead king's body as it was lowered from the *Maid of Kent* into a railway van, only the town's porters in their distinctive uniforms. 'It was carried off to Windsor with as much ceremony as Her Majesty's mails,' the *Dover Express* newspaper reported. On arrival at Windsor, however, the coffin was welcomed with great ceremonial.

Prince Arthur,
Duke of Connaught

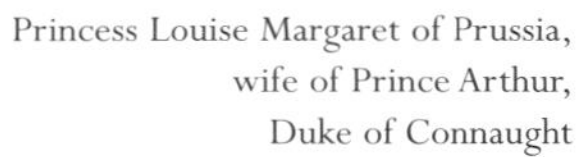
Princess Louise Margaret of Prussia,
wife of Prince Arthur,
Duke of Connaught

## Duke of Connaught

Prince Arthur, the Duke of Connaught and a son of Queen Victoria, served as a young officer in the Dover Garrison and lived in Waterloo Crescent on the sea front. In 1878 he accompanied Princess Louise Margaret of Prussia and her father, Prince Frederick Charles, from Ostend to Dover where a guard of honour greeted them. After lunch at the Lord Warden Hotel they boarded a special train for Windsor. In 1883 he and his duchess came to Dover and opened the hall and park named after him.

## More harbour improvement schemes

There were more than ten major schemes proposed for improving Dover's harbour in the years between 1865 and the end of the century. These included a completely new harbour on the west side of Admiralty Pier (an idea resurrected again in 2000 called Westport) with a complementary new port on the French coast; another envisaged ships able to carry entire trains (which did not materialise until 1936); yet another was for a Channel bridge, comprising a causeway across the Channel wide enough to take traffic but leaving a narrow strip through which ships could pass; plus, of course, a Channel tunnel scheme. One scheme jumped all the hurdles and was approved by parliament in 1883, but not because of the urgent need for a deep water refuge for shipping in general, nor to provide a coaling station for warships, or to provide for larger cross-Channel vessels, but primarily to provide 16 years work for many convicts! This and all the others failed to materialise either for lack of finance, for competing vested interests, or bickering between Dover town and the government as well as the lack of deep water at Calais preventing a fixed timetabled service.

Calais opened its new deep water harbour in 1889, whilst passengers disembarked at Dover on a wet and inconvenient Admiralty Pier with seas in rough weather sweeping right over the quay, drenching everybody.

A busy harbour in 1898

Commercial harbour proposals, 1890

## William Crundall

The very existence of Dover Harbour Board came under threat in the 1880s. William Crundall, a Dover timber merchant and a Conservative, was appointed to the Harbour Board as a Board of Trade representative in 1885 and, anxious to see improvements, quickly became a thorn in the side of the Liberal Lord Granville, Lord Warden and Chairman. Amazingly, when a Liberal government regained power in 1886, Crundall was replaced by a Liberal from Shropshire. This was unprecedented. Appointments were always for life. Despite uproar in parliament, the decision was not changed. Crundall then became Mayor of Dover, an office he was to hold a record 13 times, and promptly drew up a parliamentary bill to transfer control of the harbour to Dover Corporation and to dissolve the Harbour Board! It almost succeeded, but was eventually withdrawn. William Crundall was reappointed to the Board in 1888 and promptly made plans for a new commercial harbour, which were approved by parliament in 1891.

William Crundall (standing) with Worsford Mowll

This new commercial harbour was nothing like the enormous harbour of refuge envisaged by the government for the Royal Navy, but would provide smooth water of some 60 acres between an extended Admiralty Pier and a new pier to the east, eventually named Prince of Wales Pier. Control of Admiralty Pier was also transferred to the Harbour Board.

## Promenade Pier

At the same time, 1891, a pleasure pier was built privately halfway along the seafront and it opened in 1893, but had a sad, short life. It never paid its way and only 18 months after completion part of it was swept away. It was popular for a time and a pavilion at the sea end was opened in 1901. Pleasure steamers plying around the Kent coast called. These were suspended in 1907, however, because of all the moorings for warships. Subsequently, the pier was sold to the Admiralty and was demolished in 1927.

Promenade Pier in 1908

The opening of the Prince of Wales Pier in 1902

# Prince of Wales Pier

On 20 July 1893 the West Riding Regiment marched down from South Front Barracks on the Western Heights to the prettily decorated Harbour Station where the mayor, Lord Warden and other dignitaries awaited the special train carrying Edward, Prince of Wales. On arrival flag signallers on the roof of the station signalled the batteries around the bay to fire the royal salute. The Prince and the rest of the party then drove off through the cheering crowds waiting in the rain, through a triumphal arch to a carpeted pavilion, containing 1500 people and with many more outside. There, in strong winds and driving rain, the Prince, using a silver trowel for the mortar and an ivory mallet, laid the first stone of the Prince of Wales Pier, watched by the high and mighty of Kent as well as dignitaries from Calais, Boulogne and Ostend. Placed under the stone were two large sealed bottles, containing some newspapers and coins with a brass plate giving the names of the Marquess of Dufferin and Ava who was Lord Warden, and Sir James Coode, the engineer. A launch attached a bugle to its engine and rather haphazardly played, '*God Bless the Prince of Wales*' to everybody's amusement. The long awaited dream of a deep water enclosed harbour would soon be a reality.

The Prince of Wales laying the foundation-stone of the Prince of Wales Pier

Unfortunately, there was some confusion as guests left in the pouring rain. People got into the wrong carriages, even some who had no right to a carriage! However, all eventually arrived safely at the Town Hall with the Prince braving the weather in an open carriage through the decorated streets. In Cannon Street 5,000 children sang *God Bless the Prince of Wales*, which had become an unofficial second national anthem. The Prince was impressed and stopped his carriage to acknowledge the children.

Prince of Wales Pier in 1908

Prince of Wales arriving by train at Admiralty Pier in 1895

Later, the children each received cake and an orange from Lady Crundall, wife of the mayor as well as a medal from George Wyndham, the local member of parliament. After a grand luncheon, the Prince drove through the grounds of Dover College where the cheers of the boys could be heard, especially after the Head Prefect requested an extra week's holiday, which the Prince granted! With yet one more rendition of *God Bless the Prince of Wales*, he departed from Priory Station.

The harbour saw two royal arrivals on the same day on 13 September 1894. The Prince of Wales arrived from Calais and the Queen of Portugal also arrived after being at the death bed of her father the Comte de Paris. Dover crowds gave the Prince of Wales a particularly hearty welcome when he disembarked in 1899 after a narrow escape when fired at from close range in Brussels.

## Construction of the great naval harbour

In 1895 the Harbour Board, having waited many years for the government to build its harbour of refuge for both commercial and naval purposes, finally started building its own smaller harbour, but was soon faced with parliament deciding at long last that a grand harbour of refuge must be built. It was much like the 1844 plan, but now had to be torpedo proof! Some 600 acres of water would be enclosed by extending the Admiralty Pier 2000 feet, building an eastern arm 3320 feet long and a southern breakwater 4200 feet long three quarters of a mile from shore. Beyond East Cliff 21 acres would be reclaimed from the sea. This new harbour would provide sufficient mooring space for 20 battleships and their accompanying destroyers and support vessels. Construction began in 1897. Because of this, some modifications were needed to the Prince of Wales Pier, which had been completed in 1902, and for a few years, whilst this incredible feat of engineering was under way, things were difficult for cross-Channel traffic.

Above: Admiralty Pier extension, 1905
Below: Eastern Arm construction, 1908

The Maharajah of Jaipur arrives

# Edward VII

Following the death of Queen Victoria in 1901, her son became king after 60 years as Prince of Wales. Largely excluded from important royal duties during these years, he was prominent in society and was cited in two divorce cases. He did encourage his mother to return to public life, however, after her long period of mourning, following the death of Albert in 1861. Important visitors, including oriental potentates, landed at Dover en route for Edward VII's coronation in 1902. The Maharajah of Jaipur arrived with 150 men by special boat from Calais. The colourful dress of these and the enormous amount of baggage all over the deck aroused the interest of the crowd on Admiralty Pier. Even more attention was given to the four very scantily clad cooks, sitting on their haunches, baking cakes over a large charcoal stove. Other cooks were mixing a curry of some sort and yet more were cleaning large brass dishes with sand and water. Amongst the baggage to come off were six enormous copper jars filled with holy water from their country. Nobody was allowed to touch them and they were guarded even in the railway van. In addition to much food, soil from the home country was unloaded so that the potentate could have it in his boots and thereby walk on his home ground!

The King of the Belgians arrived on his yacht *Alberta* on 18 July in the same year. This was not to attend the coronation as it was customary for crowned heads not to attend coronations. He took a look round Dover and then went on to Cowes to visit the King convalescing after appendicitis which had caused postponement of the coronation. Similarly, the Shah of Persia arrived in August with a large retinue. He drove to Kearsney, just outside Dover, and back through the town with a mounted escort.

# Entente Cordiale

During Edward VII's reign Great Britain sought the friendship of France and Russia to combat the growing threat from the Kaiser's Germany. On 6 July 1903, the Duke of Connaught, on behalf of his brother, Edward VII, received President Loubet of France when he landed at the Prince of Wales Pier, escorted by the French Fleet and received by the British Fleet. No expense was spared and a large pavilion was erected specially on the pier. With all the streets decorated and lined with troops, the party then drove in open carriages along the sea front to Market Square and on to Priory Station to take the train to London. The Entente Cordiale was signed in 1904 between the two countries and on 25 May 1908 Prince Arthur of Connaught – who had been greeted himself when he arrived at Dover on the *Lord Warden* in December 1904, following a visit to Italy – met French President Fallières at the Prince of Wales Pier when he arrived for a state visit in the French warship *Leon Gambetta* to the sound of a 21 gun salute, having steamed through two lines of battleships moored between Shakespeare Cliff and Dover Pier. In a specially erected pavilion on the pier he received an address from the Mayor and Corporation and then the party processed in carriages through the town to Priory Station. He departed for France four days later, but in the interval the 14,500 sailors of the French and British fleets in port for the occasion were entertained in the decorated town. There was an evening fête in Connaught Park with a firework display, smoking concerts, an athletics competition and a banquet at the Lord Warden Hotel. Bands played on the sea front, which was illuminated, and warships were open to the public.

Admiralty Pier in 1904

# Visits by Edward VII

Edward VII's first visit to Dover as King was on 6 April 1905 when, surprisingly, there was little pomp and ceremony with no military reception or naval escort but only a civic reception. The King was en route to join his wife, Queen Alexandra, who was in Marseilles on the royal yacht, *Victoria and Albert*. Despite the private nature and short notice of the visit, the Dover Corporation, the Harbour Board, the railway company and the military combined to put on a good show! The Admiralty Pier was brightly decorated by Flashman & Co. including the best flowers that Covent Garden could supply! The railway line from Harbour Station to the Admiralty Pier was also decorated and ships in harbour, as well as buildings in the town, were covered in bunting. Security was tight with both soldiers and police marshalling the crowds. Every bridge that the King's train went under was also guarded and plain clothes policemen mingled with the crowd. The Corporation walked in their robes from the Lord Warden Hotel as the royal train made its way along the Admiralty Pier. The Deputy Mayor welcomed his majesty as he alighted from the train and then quickly boarded *The Queen*, which was to take him across the Channel, raising his hat as he did so to the cheering crowds. Harbour Board tugs, the *Lady Curzon* and the *Lady Vita* were ready to assist the ship's departure in the heavy swell, but they were not needed. The King left only 10 minutes after the train's arrival, but not without him noticing an elderly man standing bareheaded in the cold wind – as required in the presence of the monarch – who was kindly told to put his hat on!

Edward VII crossed the Channel from Dover several times during his reign. One such occasion was on 4 May 1905 when he was on board the new vessel, *Onward*, when it began service on the Dover/Calais route. Initially he used the Admiralty Pier. His train would be seen approaching from Shakespeare Cliff tunnel by crowds assembled on

Edward VII being greeted at Dover

Train on Wellington Bridge 1910

Admiralty Pier. The King would step out on to the red-carpeted platform and footmen would follow him with Caesar, his favourite terrier. Men would raise their hats and cheer as he boarded a special steamer, pausing to greet the mayor and others assembled. The ship would cast off immediately. Later, he preferred the greater privacy of the Prince of Wales Pier, which meant that the royal train had to pass slowly through the old Pier District of Dover on to the pier. This change was caused, apparently, by cameras having been stuck in his face previously! He departed from this pier for the first time on 10 August 1908 when he used the new royal yacht, *Alexandra*, also for the first time, en route for Marienbad, where he took the health waters every year; although on this occasion he was also meeting the German and Austrian emperors.

## Transatlantic liners

*Deutschland* at Prince of Wales Pier, 1904

Transatlantic German liners were persuaded to call at Dover from 1 July 1904, mooring on the east side of the Prince of Wales Pier. This created an urgent need for a rail connection to the end of the pier. A temporary solution was built in five months and was never replaced. This ran from the Harbour Station along Strond Street and Union Quay over the Wellington swing bridge, across the Esplanade to the pier, where a small station was built. Within a year five companies were calling. More berthing facilities were needed, but the Admiralty opposed any more interference with their activities. However, a compromise was reached – once the Naval Harbour was completed, the Harbour Board would have exclusive use of the whole of the Admiralty Pier and the navy would have sole use of the Prince of Wales Pier, confining commercial shipping between the two piers. This urgent need for more facilities for liner traffic was shortlived. Currents at the western entrance caused difficulties for the large liners and damage to the *Deutschland* in 1906 was a turning point as one liner company after another pulled out of Dover over the next few years.

Dover seafront,
early 20th century

## 1906 Act of Parliament

The Lord Warden was relieved of the automatic chairmanship of the Harbour Board by Act of Parliament in 1906, when George, Prince of Wales, held the post; William Crundall, local business man, councillor and many times mayor, became chairman and remained so until his death in 1934.

Prince of Wales, later George V
in Dover, 1909

## Completion of the Admiralty Harbour

In 1909 the building of the great Admiralty Harbour was completed and to mark this historic event, which was to have such an impact upon Dover and its harbour, the Prince of Wales, later George V, unveiled a commemorative stone on 15 October. He arrived by special train and was received on the Esplanade by the Admiral Commander in Chief of the Nore and the General Commanding Eastern Command as royal salutes were fired from the castle and ships in harbour. The robed Mayor and Corporation presented the Prince with an address of welcome on illuminated vellum enclosed in a silver gilt frame. The Prince handed over a written reply before inspecting the Northumberland Fusiliers' guard of honour. Escorted by 11th Hussars, the royal party moved off to East Cliff with the route lined by troops and bands playing, making a brilliant spectacle for the crowds. The stone laying took place in a beautifully decorated, special pavilion at the shore end of the eastern arm. There the Prince was greeted by a naval guard of honour and by the Lords of the Admiralty, the Archbishop of Canterbury, the Lord Warden and the High Sheriff of Kent. Watched by 450 seated dignitaries, the Prince was presented with a book on the history of the construction. A casket was placed underneath where the stone was to be laid. Inside was a parchment recording the construction with some coins, copies of local newspapers and a copy of *The Times*. The Prince then laid the mortar on top of the casket and the stone was lowered into place. After driving along the sea front, he boarded a train at the Clock Tower, which took him along the

Harbour, 1905

Admiralty Pier to the *Enchantress*, an Admiralty yacht, where he lunched with the Lords of the Admiralty and other guests. He left by train from the Prince of Wales Pier station later in the afternoon to yet more royal salutes.

No great fleet of warships was ever based in this great harbour, which had taken 70 years to materialise. Buoys intended for 66 warships were laid, but insufficient shelter meant ships rolled in heavy weather and so the navy made far less use of it than planned, much to the dismay of Dover tradesmen.

## Marine Station

During the same year, 1909, widening of the Admiralty Pier at its shore end began in order to provide over 11 acres for the long planned marine station. This was designed to cope with up to four trains simultaneously. Unfortunately, the old 1847 Pilot House had to be removed to make way for the approach to the station.

Marine Station
completed in 1914

Queen Alexandra at Dover

## Death of Edward VII

Edward VII died in 1910 just two weeks after arriving back in Dover following recuperation in Biarritz. His queen, Alexandra, returned via Dover only a day before he died. Having been somewhat wayward as Prince of Wales, he proved to be an effective and popular monarch. His death in May brought many foreign royal arrivals to Dover Harbour – normal ferries were used as specials but also the royal yacht *Alexandra*.

George V, standing centre, at Dover

## George V

The new king, George V, had first crossed the Channel, aged four and a half, in January 1869 with his father, Edward, Prince of Wales and his sister, Princess Victoria. Whilst Prince of Wales, he was Lord Warden briefly in 1906-7, although he was never installed in the traditional manner.

In 1913 President Poincaré of France arrived as the guest of George V and left from the Prince of Wales Pier on 27 June after an address from the Recorder, Sir A Bodkin KCB in the presence of the Mayor and Corporation. The large number of French and British warships in the harbour made an impressive sight and as the President departed three aircraft flew overhead – a rare sight only four years after Bleriot had flown across the Channel for the first time.

Early in 1914 George V and Queen Mary visited Paris. They arrived at the Prince of Wales Pier by train and embarked on the royal yacht. At Calais they boarded their own railway coach, which was stored at Calais for such occasions.

Warships in harbour during World War I

## First World War

Britain's gateway to the continent slammed shut on the outbreak of war on 4 August 1914 when Dover's cross-Channel services were suspended. The First World War meant that Dover and its harbour was not only busy as the nearest port to the continent for embarking troops and supplies, receiving the wounded and the dead, it was also the base for the Dover Patrol, which guarded shipping in the Channel and carried out raids against the occupied Belgian coast. The Marine Station was quickly finished and 13 ambulance trains, making 3 trips a day, coped with the wounded arriving on nine hospital ships a day. Two ships with antisubmarine and torpedo nets suspended between them were sunk to block the western entrance of the harbour. They remained in place until 1931 when one was removed and the other moved but marked with a buoy. Dover and its harbour was also in the front line itself, bombed frequently by enemy aircraft and by shells fired from the French coast.

Submarines in the Granville Dock, World War I

On 23 September 1915 George V, in the uniform of an Admiral of the Fleet, arrived at the Prince of Wales Pier and then went by naval launch to Promenade Pier, where he got into an open car accompanied by Admiral Sir Reginald Bacon in command at Dover. He visited the dockyard and naval establishment and had lunch with the Admiral and his officers. After visiting the Admiral's offices at Fleet House in Marine Parade, he drove to the naval aerodrome at the top of Castle Hill and then to Capel aerodrome. Large crowds cheered him wherever he went. Later that year, on 1 November, circumstances were very different when the King was brought in to Dover on the hospital ship *Anglia* from Boulogne and then went by hospital train to London. His horse had rolled on him whilst inspecting troops in France and he was badly injured. This was not made known at the time. During the Great War George V changed his family's name from the German Saxe Coburg to the very English name of Windsor.

The harbour witnessed the departure of the Dover Patrol on 22 April 1918 to seal German submarines in the canals at Zeebrugge. The next day, after the Zeebrugge Raid, crowds cheered and every ship in the harbour paid homage as the battered cruiser, *HMS Vindictive*, limped into harbour. The raid cost 156 lives and 400 wounded. Later the same year a disaster for the harbour and the town was narrowly averted, although at great human cost. In August a large fleet was assembled in the harbour to recapture the Flanders coast. Suddenly, there was a tremendous explosion on the battleship, *Glatton*, killing or injuring many of its crew. With unexploded ammunition on board and ammunition ships close by, *Glatton* was a danger to all the other ships, to the harbour and to the town. The difficult decision was taken to torpedo the vessel, trapping 58 on board. *Glatton* became their grave. The vessel was not lifted until 1926.

*HMS Vindictive* after the Zeebrugge Raid (Courtesy of the Imperial War Museum, London, ref Q18887)

The King was in Dover three times in 1918, twice on his way to visit the armies in France and on 27 November to visit Paris with the Prince of Wales and Prince Albert, who later became George VI. The public were not allowed on Admiralty Pier, but crammed the footbridge over the railway line between Marine Station and the Lord Warden Hotel to cheer the King. After being greeted by Vice Admiral Keyes and the mayor, the destroyer, *Broke*, famous for sinking two German destroyers off Dover in 1917, took the royal party across the Channel escorted by six battleships, seaplanes and aircraft.

German postcard showing aircraft attacking the harbour

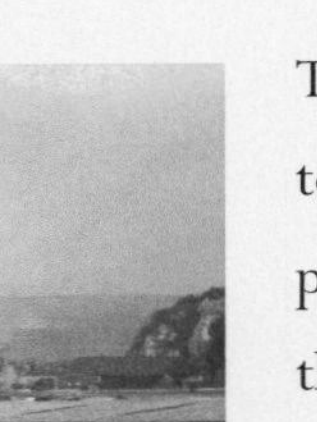

Upturned wreck of *HMS Glatton*

## Armistice and prisoners of war come home

The War ended on 11 November 1918 and on 17 November the Prince of Wales, later Edward VIII, came to Dover for a very happy occasion when he welcomed the return of the first prisoners of war. The ex prisoners, dressed in new uniforms and looking much better than when they were first released in rags by the Germans, arrived in the *ss France* to warships sounding their sirens, whistles from railway engines and the cheers from soldiers and civilians. The excited crowd even stormed the Marine Station to get a better view. A band played *Pack Up Your Troubles In Your Old Kit Bag* as the men were drawn up by the Custom House where the Prince of Wales read a speech of welcome from the King and Queen watched by Vice Admiral Sir Roger Keyes and the wartime mayor, Edwin Farley. Before the Prince had finished, the band struck up *God Save the King!* The Prince then welcomed the men himself before they were supplied with refreshments and, cheered to the echo, were taken in lorries, ambulances and cars to their quarters in a Dover barracks. Some were carrying souvenirs of German sausage and black bread. Those who were fit were soon sent on two months leave and the remainder went to hospital. One Dover family was especially happy; amongst those returning was a Dover soldier reported killed.

Duke of Connaught greets President Wilson at Dover

## President Woodrow Wilson

The first visit to Britain by an American president whilst in office occurred in 1918 when President Woodrow Wilson and his wife arrived at Admiralty Pier on Boxing Day in *ss Brighton*, after being escorted across the Channel by destroyers and aircraft. Surrounded by many U.S. and British officials, he was met by the Duke of Connaught, Admiral Sir Roger Keyes and the Mayor and Corporation with an address from the Recorder signed by the mayor, Edwin Farley and the town clerk, R E Knocker. The Dover crowd gave the president a tremendous ovation as he inspected the naval guard of honour on the pier before leaving by train for London from Marine Station. On 31 December he returned to France from Dover.

Fishing boats on the Crosswall, 1920

## Normal service resumed

Civilian cross-Channel services resumed in 1919 and soon some liners were calling. The Harbour Board had lost most of its revenue during the war and the rundown harbour took time to recover. However, there were plans to improve and enlarge the tidal harbour; the railways wanted to improve their facilities around the inner docks which would involve considerable demolition of property and the town was thinking of converting the Admiralty dockyard at the eastern end of the harbour into its own commercial port.

## Private and state visits

The first monarch to arrive by air in this country was the King of Belgians when his seaplane landed in Dover Harbour on 15 May, 1919. He was on a private visit. His predecessor was often in Dover and could be seen walking its streets and sea front.

Many other foreign royals arrived and departed from Dover on private or official visits. With the coming of the railway members of the British royal family did not always come to Dover to greet or see them off, but performed this duty at the London railway station.

King George V and Queen Mary were in Dover several times after the war. On 8 May 1922 they arrived from London at the Marine Station and were met by the Lord Lieutenant of Kent, Marquess Camden, the Lord Warden, Earl Beauchamp and the Mayor, R J Barwick, and Corporation before embarking at Admiralty Pier on the royal yacht for a state visit to Belgium and to see the war graves, returning a few days later. In March 1925 the King, accompanied by Queen Mary, sailed from Dover to recuperate from influenza and bronchitis in the Mediterranean, returning at the end of April. Later in the year they travelled via Dover in the *Biarritz* for a state visit to Italy.

George V and Queen Mary at Dover

The Royal Navy hands over its harbour to Dover Harbour Board in 1923

## Dover Harbour Board takes over the naval harbour

The war had demonstrated that under frequent attack from the air as well as shelling by warships, the harbour was obviously unsuitable as a naval base. In September 1923 the naval base and harbour was handed over to Dover Harbour Board and part of the dockyard was leased for shipbreaking.

## Improved rail and road access

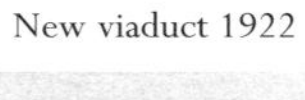

New viaduct 1922

The Harbour Board dropped its own plans but the railways, now combined to form Southern Railway, constructed a wide approach to the harbour, including a goods yard on the Shakespeare Cliff side of Admiralty Pier. Part of Henry VIII's Archcliffe Fort had to be demolished in 1926 to make way for it and the old wooden trestles supporting the railway across Shakespeare Beach were replaced by a solid embankment. Most of the Harbour Station was demolished in 1929. Road access was also improved in 1922 with the building of a 60 foot wide viaduct connecting Limekiln Street with Admiralty Pier and the Marine Station, overcoming frustrating delays at level crossings. Quays around the Wellington Dock were improved in 1929 when Northampton Quay and Commercial Quay were levelled.

Aerial ropeway emerges through the White Cliffs

## Kent Coal

With the development of the East Kent Coalfield, coal became an important export from Dover. A novel transport system, cheaper than conventional rail, was built by Richard Tilden Smith, owner of Tilmanstone Colliery. Inaugurated in 1930 it comprised an aerial ropeway – or rather wireway – with tubs each containing 3/4 ton from Tilmanstone to the Eastern Arm, where a 5,000 ton bunker received the 3,000 tons of coal a day after its 7 miles and 1 1/2 hour journey. Coal from Snowdown and Betteshanger collieries travelled conventionally via the sea front railway, built by the Admiralty during the war, from Western Docks to the Eastern Arm. With strong objections to smoke belching from the engine and the

Aerial ropeway and coal bunker, Eastern Arm, 1930

coal dust, coal traffic ceased to use this sea front railway after some years. After the Second World War it was rarely used, but the occasional sight of six trucks being pulled by a diesel engine preceded by a man walking with a red flag always attracted interest on the sea front. It was closed in 1964.

*Forde* loading by crane

## Cross-Channel competition

At the same time there were dramatic developments in cross-Channel travel. In 1928 Captain Townsend, resenting the high cost of transporting his car by Southern Railway ferry to Calais, started trading as Townsend Brothers (Shipping) Limited using a coal carrier, the *Artificer*, during the summer months to carry 15 cars with 12 drivers at half the price. Southern Railway responded quickly with fast cargo boats carrying cars only. Townsend went one better in 1930 with the *Forde*, a former minesweeper, which could carry 165 people and 26 cars, enabling the driver and his passengers to travel on the same ship for the first time. SR responded with their own new car ferry, *Autocarrier*, in 1931. Loading by crane was still slow and cumbersome.

Train ferry in Ferry Dock

## Train ferry

Travel by rail also saw improvements. The famous Golden Arrow Pullman service began in 1929 which used a specially built ship, *Canterbury*, which was the last word in luxury. Ferries able to carry not only train passengers but the train as well had been thought of way back in 1865 and had been introduced at Richborough and Southampton during the war to carry supplies to the continent. Three new ferries, *Twickenham Ferry*, *Hampton Ferry* and *Shepperton Ferry* were built to carry 12 sleeping cars or 40 wagons as well as some cars and a special dock to handle them was completed in 1936 between South Pier and Admiralty Pier. A year later these ferries also became the first drive on, drive off car ferries. The London to Paris Night Ferry through train became an instant success used by the rich and famous.

King and Queen of Rumania arrive, 1924

King and Queen of Italy arrive escorted by the Prince of Wales, 1924

## Edward, Prince of Wales

Edward, Prince of Wales visited Dover several times during the 1920s. In 1921 he greeted King Albert of the Belgians at Marine Station, who was on his way to visit George V. In 1922 the Prince unveiled the Dover Patrol Memorial at Leathercote Point on the White Cliffs and in 1924 greeted the King and Queen of Romania and the King and Queen of Italy. The royal train brought the Prince of Wales to Dover again in July 1927 to welcome Kind Fuad of Egypt. The Prince had a long wait and took his time inspecting the Royal Navy guard of honour on the quayside. Eventually, four destroyers escorted the *Maid of Orleans*, which was flying the Egyptian flag, into harbour as the 21-gun salute boomed from the castle. The Prince of Wales went on board, but the Mayor and Corporation gave the customary welcome in the Marine Station. Few saw the King land – only the passengers who had recently boarded the *Maid of Kent*. However, there were more people in the station – by invitation – and a large crowd outside the station saw the royal train leave with a squadron of aircraft escorting the train at low altitude all the way to London.

The Prince was back in Dover later in 1927 to greet the French president and in 1928 he welcomed the King of Afghanistan. As Colonel-in-Chief of the Seaforth Highlanders he arrived at Marine Station to visit them in their Dover barracks on 27 June 1929 and came again in 1933 and 1935; although in 1935 he flew in! On 10 July 1930 he arrived by plane at Swingate and drove to the Wellington Dock for the launching ceremony of the new lifeboat *Sir William Hillary*, named after the founder of the Royal National Lifeboat Institution. The Prince was President of the RNLI at the time. This new boat for the volunteer crew could travel 156 miles without refuelling and could carry 200 people if necessary. It was also the first to be fitted with wireless.

King Fuad of Egypt at Dover, 1927

Western Docks, 1932



# Duke of Kent

The Duke of Kent, a son of George V, was another visitor to Dover. He had opened the new County School for Boys buildings off Astor Avenue on 9 December 1931, but in 1934 there was a much more personal reason for coming to Dover. On 21 November he welcomed his bride-to-be, Princess Marina, who arrived with her parents, Prince and Princess Nicholas of Greece, on the *Canterbury*. On the pier were the Lord Warden, the Marquess of Reading, the Lord Lieutenant, the Mayor, Alderman G M Norman, and the Corporation.

George, Duke of Kent (right)
a son of George V.
He was later to die in an air crash

# Princess Royal

In 1934 the Princess Royal, sister of George V, visited the Royal Scots Guards as Colonel in Chief. She arrived at Marine Station and drove to Citadel Barracks. This visit was repeated on 17 June 1936, but without public ceremony as the royal court was in mourning for George V.

# Death of George V

Britain and its Empire celebrated the Silver Jubilee – 25 years on the throne – of King George V in 1935, but early in 1936 he died. Dover harbour was soon busy with arrivals for his funeral on 28 January.

Edward VIII, when Prince of Wales,
visiting the Seaforth Highlanders in Dover

# Edward VIII and the abdication crisis

Edward VIII, who succeeded his father, had visited Dover many times officially as Prince of Wales. He had also made many private visits, arriving by car or passing through the port on boat and train. This very popular prince always attracted large crowds. The new king's desire to marry Wallis Simpson, an American divorcee, precipitated a crisis – not because she was American, but because she was divorced. Having to choose between the throne and the woman he loved, he abdicated in favour of his younger brother, the Duke of York, who became King George VI before the end of 1936.

George VI at Dover in 1938

# George VI

King George VI and Queen Elizabeth arrived at Marine Station on 19 July 1938. Amongst the welcoming party was Mayor Cairns and Captain John Iron, the well-known Harbour Master, who saw them safely aboard the Admiralty Yacht *Enchantress*, which took them to Boulogne en route for Paris and a State visit. Thousands had gathered at Dover to see them leave, but dense fog prevented a view except for those privileged to be in the Marine Station. The royal couple returned in brilliant weather on 22 July and this time the crowds had a good view.

The bombing of *HMS Codrington* and *HMS Sandhurst* in the harbour, 1940

## Second World War

Following Germany's invasion of Poland, Great Britain declared war on Germany on 3 September 1939. The Harbour Board had not given the Admiralty Harbour much attention since the transfer in 1923 and now it was needed once again as a base for the Dover Patrol. Vice Admiral Ramsay, in command at Dover, was appalled at its condition and its defences. The harbour was dredged immediately. Once again Dover's ferry services were suspended and transferred to Folkestone. The eastern entrance was protected by a boom and antisubmarine net, but the western entrance remained open.

On 10 December 1939 *HMS Codrington* took George VI from Dover to France and back. This ship was bombed in the harbour during 1940 and lay ashore off Waterloo Crescent until it was towed away to be broken up in 1947. The King was in Dover again on 7 March 1940, arriving by special train. Dressed in naval uniform he went straight to the headquarters of the Dover Patrol and inspected crews and vessels of the antisubmarine and minesweeping flotillas in the harbour. Accompanied by Vice Admiral Ramsay he inspected the WRNS – the Women's Royal Naval Service - parading for the first time in their new uniforms. He was piped aboard *HMS Hampton*, a commandeered ferry, where he saw how mines were stowed and also watched a mine laying demonstration. Then he visited the Boom Defence Party on the Eastern Arm and went on to the castle to see the underground galleries and tunnels, some dating from Napoleonic times, which had been converted into a naval command centre.

August 1940. Dive-bombing Dover. Highly imaginative Italian depiction showing German Stukas attacking the harbour

George VI and Queen Elizabeth at Marine Station in 1940

Dunkirk troops glad to be back in Dover

## Dunkirk

It was in the underground caverns of Castle Cliff where Admiral Ramsay masterminded the evacuation of Dunkirk just a few months later. This was Operation Dynamo in which 338,000 troops were rescued from Dunkirk by 900 vessels of every description – from naval ships and ferries to yachts and rowing boats. During the nine day operation one quarter of the vessels were lost. Many of the soldiers were landed at Dover. Up to 60 ships a day were tied up in harbour and 327 special trains took the troops inland. With German guns only 20 miles away Dover and its harbour was shelled constantly. The capture of the harbour would be an early target for any invasion force. The western entrance was blocked again and was not reopened until 1963. The harbour was soon enveloped with barrage balloons in the air and concrete pillboxes on the ground.

In 1944, prior to the D-Day Normandy landings, the harbour was gradually filled with dummy ships made of wood and canvas floating on barrels to deceive the Germans as to where the landings would take place. The Germans fell for it. The allies did not take the shortest route across the Channel!

A packed ship arrives at Dover from Dunkirk

## Royal visit to Hellfire Corner

Following the biggest pounding by German guns in August and September 1944, the King with Queen Elizabeth visited Dover again on 18 October 1944, arriving by royal train at Kearsney just outside Dover, for a four hour visit as a tribute to Dover's fortitude during four years of shelling and bombing. Not for nothing was it known as 'hellfire corner.' With cheering people everywhere, they saw shattered homes, the air raid shelters and caves, air raid wardens' and first aid posts, listened to people's stories and saw Civil Defence workers on parade. At the Town Hall they met some of the people who had stayed on in the town, many of whom were homeless and living in the chalk caves.

George VI and Queen Elizabeth at Dover, 1944
©KM Newspapers

September 1944
People leaving the caves at Dover where they had sheltered from German long range guns across the Channel, after the Allied advance in France had captured the area from which the Germans had been firing.

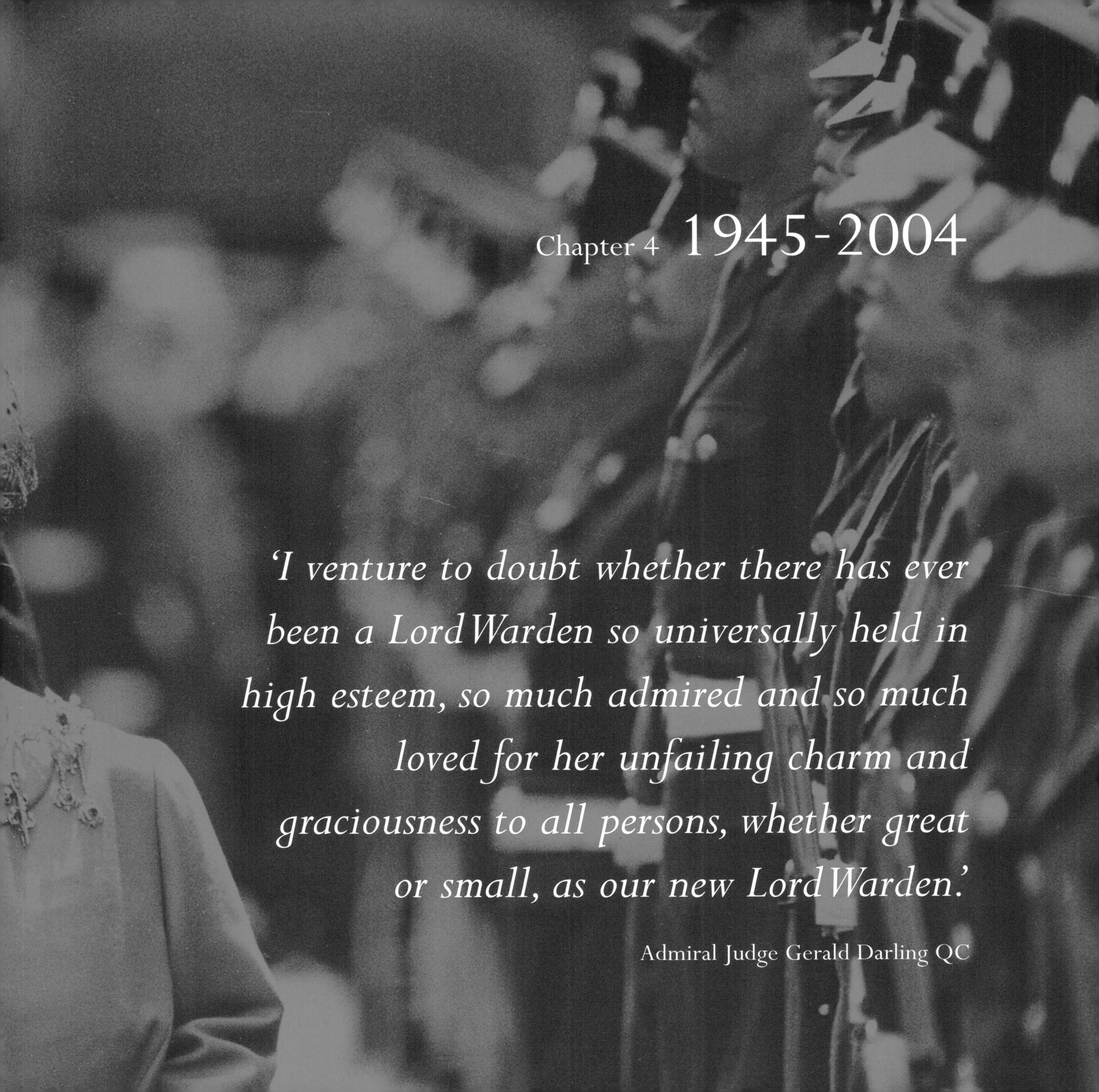

# Chapter 4 1945-2004

*'I venture to doubt whether there has ever been a Lord Warden so universally held in high esteem, so much admired and so much loved for her unfailing charm and graciousness to all persons, whether great or small, as our new Lord Warden.'*

Admiral Judge Gerald Darling QC

When the war ended in 1945 the harbour saw thousands of troops returning home to Britain and many refugees leaving for their Belgium homeland.

Duke of Windsor, formerly Edward VIII

## Duke of Windsor

The former Edward VIII, who was created Duke of Windsor following his abdication in 1936, landed in Dover with the Duchess, the former Mrs Wallis Simpson, on 11 October 1945 to make a private visit to his mother, Queen Mary, widow of George V. The Duke had served as Governor of the Bahamas from 1940 to 1945. They came again in October 1946, arriving on the *Canterbury* over two hours late due to train delays in France. The inevitable battery of press photographers were still waiting for them! Several such visits were made to Britain from their home in France until his mother died.

## Drive on, drive off ferry and inner docks enclosed

*Halladale* in 1955

Most of the harbour was handed back to the Harbour Board in September 1945 and the Royal Navy moved out completely in November 1946. Ferries returned gradually, initially carrying troops on leave. The *Canterbury* returned after distinguished war service and resumed the Golden Arrow service in April 1946. Southern Railway's *Autocarrier* resumed service and Townsend's *Forde* also returned from war service in 1947, but was replaced in 1950 by a former frigate, *Halladale*, which could carry 350 passengers and 60 cars. This became the first drive on, drive off car ferry in 1951 but only at Calais!

During this period Dover Harbour Board took steps to enclose the inner docks and provide more quay space. By 1954 Custom House Quay and the Crosswall were closed to the public. Northampton Street and the south side of Snargate Street were demolished and Strond Street had been realigned with some loss of property.

Queen Juliana arrives, 1950



## Countess Mountbatten

The President of the Royal National Lifeboat Institution, Countess Mountbatten, wife of Lord Louis Mountbatten of Burma – visited the harbour on 16 September 1949 to name Dover's new lifeboat, *Southern Africa*. Lord Mountbatten's nephew, Prince Philip, had married the King's daughter, Princess Elizabeth, in 1947 and was created Duke of Edinburgh.

## Queen Juliana and Prince Bernhard

Queen Juliana was the first reigning sovereign of the Netherlands to arrive in Dover when she came on 21 November 1950 with her husband, Prince Bernhard, to begin a four day state visit. She crossed the Channel in a Dutch cruiser and was escorted by a British destroyer. Outside the harbour *HMS Cleopatra* fired a 21 gun salute and another royal salute was fired from the castle as the ships entered harbour, watched by crowds on the Prince of Wales Pier. With the vessel tied up on Admiralty Pier, the Queen inspected Dutch marines on board, disembarked and then inspected the British guard of honour on the quay. She was welcomed by the Duke of Gloucester on behalf of King George VI, his brother. In the Marine Station special stands had been erected where the mayor and mayoress, Councillor W. H. Fish and his wife, greeted the royal couple officially, recalling that the Queen had stayed in Britain during the Second World War with her mother, Queen Wilhelmina. In her reply Queen Juliana said that she was 'proud to come ashore at the most exposed and battered bastion of the free world.' The royal party then left for London by train, waving to the crowds from the compartment window.

The Duke of Gloucester accompanying Queen Juliana and Prince Bernhard

The Duke of Edinburgh accompanying the King and Queen of Denmark

## King and Queen of Denmark

Danish monarchs usually arrived at Harwich when visiting Britain, but for their four day state visit in May 1951 King Frederick and Queen Ingrid landed at Dover to be greeted by thousands of Dovorians, despite the biting wind and heavy rain. Escorted by British naval ships and RAF aircraft, their harbour approach was announced by a 21 gun salute from the battleship *HMS Vanguard*. As soon as the *Kronprincesse Ingrid* berthed at the Admiralty Pier, the Duke of Edinburgh went on board. As the royal party inspected the guard of honour made up from the Royal Navy and The Buffs – King Frederick was Colonel-in-Chief of The Buffs and honorary admiral of the Royal Navy – the Royal Marines' band played the Danish national anthem. A thoughtful touch was that Queen Ingrid was wearing a diamond-studded brooch, depicting The Buffs badge. Following the customary address of welcome from the Mayor of Dover and the reply from the King, the royal party left by train with the royal arms of Denmark on the front of the engine.

Busy ferry berths in the 1960s

## Car Ferry Terminal

In 1952 passengers through Dover reached two million, exceeding the 1939 total for the first time. With more and more car traffic – 40,000 in 1948 and over 200,000 in 1955 – cars were being loaded at Admiralty Pier, Train Ferry Dock and by the Camber with complaints about delays, poor access and antiquated methods. There was an urgent need for a proper car terminal. The Eastern Docks Car Ferry Terminal duly opened in 1953, including two purpose-built ferry berths with drive on, drive off facilities, a large Customs examination shed, car parks and restaurants.

*Compiegne and Dinard*, 1958

## Harbour Board reorganisation

The constitution of the Harbour Board had been changed again in 1938 to eight members and in 1956 comprised one from the Ministry of Defence, two from the Ministry of Transport, three from British Rail and two from Dover Borough Council.

## King Faisal of Iraq

There was a colourful scene in the harbour in 1956 when the 21 year old King Faisal of Iraq, who had crossed the Channel in *HMS Defender*, arrived for a four day state visit. Special stands and enclosures had been erected on the quayside and the crowds gave him a warm welcome as he stepped ashore. Twenty-three years earlier his grandfather had stood on the same spot. The band of the Royal West Kent Regiment played whilst guns boomed from the castle and aircraft dipped their wings in salute. Ships, dressed over all, blew their whistles and hooters amid cheers from dock workers. The scarlet and gold bunting on Marine Station platforms was matched by the splendid gold and blue uniform of the young king. He was met by a bemedalled Duke of Gloucester on behalf of his niece, the Queen, and was welcomed by the mayor. The Chairman of Dover Harbour Board, Mr H T Hawksfield, and Mr Byford, the General Manager, were amongst the welcoming party.

King Faisal inspecting the guard of honour

## Queen Elizabeth, the Queen Mother

The next year the harbour saw another grand occasion, but for a very different reason. On 5 July 1957 Queen Elizabeth the Queen Mother, as George VI's widow was known following his death in 1952, arrived from Saltwood Castle where she had spent the night. The Duke of Gloucester also arrived after spending the night in Dover Castle. They boarded the destroyer, *HMS Chieftain*, which took them to Dunkirk to unveil the Dunkirk Memorial – a tribute to the 68,000 men who had died in the 1940 evacuation which had saved 338,000 men from the enemy. Hundreds of important guests witnessed the occasion from specially erected enclosures and there was a great send off from 50 little ships of all types, reminiscent of Dunkirk, lining the way out of the harbour. The royal party returned the same evening to another large welcoming crowd.

France. 1957.
The Queen Mother
is pictured during her visit
to Dunkirk

Queen Elizabeth inspects the Gordon Highlanders outside Dover Town Hall, 1958

## Queen Elizabeth II

The first official peacetime visit to the town of Dover by a reigning monarch for 115 years occurred in 1958. The young Queen Elizabeth II paid her first visit to Dover on 4 April when she and her husband, the Duke of Edinburgh, arrived on the royal yacht, *Britannia*, following a four day state visit to the Netherlands. The first craft to welcome *Britannia* as she entered harbour was the Dover lifeboat, *Southern Africa*, followed by the Harbour Board's brand new tug, *Dominant*, and her sister ship, *Diligent*. An armada of small craft followed the yacht in. A 21 gun royal salute was fired from the castle and a jet fighter flew overhead, whilst whistles and sirens from ships dressed over all joined the cheers of crowds from shops and factories that had closed for the occasion. The Queen was piped from the yacht into the special pavilion built by the Harbour Board where she was greeted by the Lord Lieutenant of Kent, Lord Cornwallis, the mayor, Alderman J Williams and the Chairman of Dover Harbour Board, Mr Hawksfield. They drove from the Prince of Wales Pier to the castle where they took in the view before driving to the Town Hall through Dover's streets lined three or four deep with cheering people, including 6,000 school children. There, spontaneous 'Kentish Fire' applause broke out as she entered the ancient building of the Maison Dieu.

*RY Britannia* enters harbour, 1958

Western Docks in the 1960s

## Industry makes way for vehicles

The rapid increase in car traffic at the Eastern Docks necessitated the removal of all the industries on the site. The long disused aerial ropeway and coal bunker were removed from the Eastern Arm in 1955; Dover Industries left in 1964 after breaking up ships for 35 years; the Parker Pen company moved out in 1968 after 20 years; the oil depot, dating back to the First World War, was gradually demolished from 1971; the Post Office cable ship depot closed in 1975 after 85 years and the naval salvage depot in 1976. These clearances allowed space for a third ferry berth in 1966. This was a double-decker allowing loading and unloading simultaneously.

SRNI arrives in 1959

# A new form of transport

The crossing of the Channel by a strange looking craft, *SRN1*, in 1959 heralded a new form of travel – by hovercraft – and in 1966 Townsend operated a 38 seater passengers only service, but it only lasted one season before being axed. Nevertheless, in 1968 five and a half acres were reclaimed in the Eastern Docks for Dover's first hoverport. In August 1968 the Queen's younger sister, Princess Margaret, with her husband, Lord Snowdon, opened the Eastern Docks Hoverport and then crossed the Channel at 70 miles per hour in British Rail's *The Princess Margaret* which could carry 30 cars and 250 passengers. Princess Anne followed her aunt in October 1969 when she named a similar hovercraft after herself and then travelled to Boulogne and back in the craft.

Eastern Docks with a new hoverport, 1968

## More and bigger ferries

Ferries were increasing in size to meet demand. The first of Townsend's Free Enterprise vessels appeared in 1962 and in 1965 *FE II*, the first drive through ferry, which enabled vehicles to drive on at one end of the ship and to drive off at the other. The first ferry designed for lorries was the *FE III* in 1966. Following the merger with Thoresen, a Norwegian company, Townsend's parent company became European Ferries. British Rail, the nationalised railway company, also introduced new vessels as did the Belgian and French railway companies. In 1969 these railway companies formed the Sealink consortium.

## Princess Marina of Kent

In July 1967 Dover had yet another new lifeboat, provided by the Ancient Order of Foresters and named *Faithful Forester*. The mother of the present Duke, Princess Marina of Kent, whose husband had been killed during the War, performed the naming ceremony.

Princess Marina, 1967

A Ray Warner photograph of
Eastern Docks in 1970

## More reclamation

The redeveloped Car Ferry Terminal opened in 1970. Reclamation of another nine and a half acres of the harbour allowed another double-decker berth to be opened at the Eastern Docks in 1973 plus a new freight assembly area. A fifth berth was added in 1975 by which time over half the harbour's passengers were using the Eastern Docks. Two new super berths were completed in 1978, built on the site of the old hoverport, plus another six acre reclamation. These could turn round ferries carrying up to 320 cars in 75 minutes by loading and unloading on two levels. This made seven ro-ro berths at Eastern Docks. With more and more freight vehicles awaiting Customs clearance another ten acres of the harbour were reclaimed for the import freight area using sand from the Goodwins. A car ferry berth was constructed on the Admiralty Pier and a new viaduct replaced the old in 1975. A third ferry operator, P&O Normandy Ferries, came to Dover in 1976 with the *Lion* soon to be joined by the *Tiger* and *Panther*.

## Prince Charles, Royal Navy

Prince Charles, Prince of Wales and heir to the throne, was a Royal Navy officer for several years. He paid a surprise visit to Dover when he sailed into the harbour on 20 May 1976 in command of *HMS Bronington*. The ship had been involved in manoeuvres in the Channel. Despite berthing at the Camber, Prince Charles did not come ashore, although local friends and relatives of the crew went on board before the vessel sailed again next morning. He did come ashore from *Bronington* the following month when he visited the coastguard station at Leathercote Point for a briefing before putting to sea to look for 'rogue' ships contravening the new one-way system in the Channel – the busiest waterway in the world.

Prince Charles in command
of *HMS Bronington*, 1976

The new hoverport at the Western Docks

# A new hoverport

By 1977 8 million passengers, 1,200,000 cars and 400,000 heavy goods vehicles were using the port. All this traffic had to go through the town centre and in 1977 the long-awaited A2 bypass with its viaduct into the Eastern Docks, Jubilee Way, opened.

Seaspeed, British Rail's hovercraft service, soon needed larger craft and more space. Instead of building new, the two existing craft were stretched to carry 400 passengers and 65 cars. After much controversy, 15 acres were reclaimed between the Prince of Wales Pier and North Pier for a new hoverport, using sand from the Goodwins. This necessitated replacing the open metalwork section of the pier by concrete. When it opened in July 1978 only the small The Princess Margaret, awaiting stretching, was present, the other was still being modified and of the two expected French craft one had not arrived and the other had been destroyed by fire! The official opening by the Duke of Kent occurred later in 1978. Whilst the surplus sand from the Goodwins dumped on the beach was a bonus for the town, the King Charles II Walk, opened in 1960, was lost and the noise of the hovercraft was quite deafening on the sea front.

Winston Churchill drives through Dover to be installed as Lord Warden, 1946

# The new Lord Warden

Perhaps the most memorable post war royal occasion for Dover and its harbour occurred in 1979 when Queen Elizabeth the Queen Mother arrived on 1 August on the royal yacht *Britannia* for her installation as Lord Warden of the Cinque Ports. Dover had not seen such pageantry for many years.

The post of Lord Warden of the Cinque Ports dates from the early 13th century. Originally the prime function was to act as admiral of the Cinque Ports' fleet in time of war, but it also provided direct communication for the king with these ports and also gave the portsmen a leader, enabling them to act together and to influence the king. From the 11th century the two primary defences for South East England were Dover Castle and the Cinque Ports' ships, originally under separate command. Hubert de Burgh, Constable (governor) of Dover Castle successfully defended the castle against the French in 1216 and in the following year took charge of the Cinque Ports' fleet and defeated the French fleet. From then on the constables were also appointed Lord Warden to ensure that the king's commands were carried out by the portsmen, but they also had to undertake to defend the charter rights and liberties of the Cinque Ports. By the end of the 14th century it became an appointment for life. Today the post is now largely ceremonial.

There were three Lord Wardens of the Cinque Ports and Constables of Dover Castle in the second half of the twentieth century. Sir Winston Churchill was offered the appointment during the Second World War, but he was far too busy to visit Dover for his installation until 1946. When he died, aged 90, he was succeeded in 1965 by Sir Robert Menzies (later Lord Menzies) who, as Prime Minister of Australia, had proved such a great ally during the war. Following Sir Robert's death everyone was delighted when the Queen appointed her mother, Elizabeth the Queen Mother, to the joint posts, the first woman in history to be made Lord Warden.

Sir Robert Menzies at Dover Castle, 1965 prior to his installation

*Britannia* arries with the new Lord Warden on board, 1979

The Queen Mother is greeted by the Lord Lieutenant of Kent

*Britannia*, escorted by the minesweepers *HMS Alfriston* and *HMS Glasserton*, arrived in driving rain and gale force winds to a 21 gun royal salute, which was almost drowned by the wind and the noise of a hovercraft! Despite the foul weather the Dover lifeboat, the Dover Harbour Board tugs, ferries dressed over all and an armada of canoeists greeted the vessel. The wind prevented *Britannia* from berthing at the Prince of Wales Pier and so the royal party came ashore by royal barge to be welcomed by Lord Astor, the Lord Lieutenant of Kent. The rest of the reception party welcomed Her Majesty at Dover Castle, including Sir Clifford Jarrett, Chairman of Dover Harbour Board and Kenneth Davis, the General Manager and Register. Accompanying the Queen Mother was Prince Edward, son of Queen Elizabeth II, the Queen Mother's daughter, Princess Margaret, with her children, Viscount Linley and Lady Sarah Armstrong-Jones. Unfortunately, Dover saw nothing of Princess Margaret who stayed on board suffering from a cold.

First came a hallowing service conducted by the Archbishop of Canterbury, Dr Donald Coggan, at the ancient church of St Mary in the Castle. Thousands, up to ten deep, crowded the decorated streets to watch 60 Household Cavalry troopers with swords drawn escort the carriage procession from Dover Castle to the Grand Court of Shepway, convened in a large marquee in the grounds of Dover College, the site of the mediaeval Priory of St Martin. At her installation the Queen Mother vowed to protect the franchises, liberties and customs of the Cinque Ports, whilst guns boomed out from the castle and the RAF flew overhead. She realised that she would also be responsible for the burial of all whales and other royal fish washed up along the Cinque Ports' coast!

Admiral Judge Gerald Darling QC gave this welcoming speech after the installation, '...a special honour that the Queen Mother is the first member of the royal family to be fully installed, and also the first lady Lord Warden. Although there have been many Lords Warden of distinction and fame, I venture to doubt whether there has ever been a Lord Warden so universally held in high esteem, so much admired and so much loved for her unfailing charm and graciousness to all persons, whether great or small, as our new Lord Warden.'

The Lord Warden processing through the grounds of Dover College, 1979

After the ancient and colourful ceremony the Queen Mother, looking radiant, walked in sunshine through the huge crowds to have lunch at the Town Hall followed by 200 delegates of the Confederation of the Cinque Ports and other guests. Typically, after inspecting the Royal Navy guard of honour, she stopped to chat to patients from the hospital. In the evening the Queen Mother held a reception on board *Britannia*, which concluded with the Royal Marines from the yacht performing the 'Beating Retreat' ceremony on the pier. Finally, as *Britannia* slipped her moorings at the end of this memorable day, a 21 gun salute accompanied a firework display as a farewell to the new Lord Warden.

Subsequently, the Queen Mother made regular visits to the Dover area, usually weekending at her official residence at Walmer Castle a few days before her birthday. Several of these visits did not involve the harbour since the Queen Mother often arrived by helicopter.

Rotary International Great Britain provided most of the money for another new Dover lifeboat called *Rotary Service*, which the Queen Mother named on 30 October 1979.

She arrived in *Britannia* once again on 9 July 1980 to start a three day visit to East Kent, visiting her Cinque Ports. Her escorts *HMS Gavinton* and *HMS Glasserton* were joined from Dungeness onwards by the Dover lifeboat, which she had named during her previous visit. Once again, it was raining hard on arrival and the reception party had to go on board to welcome her as the royal salute of 21 guns boomed out from the castle. The itinerary included a meeting of the Confederation of the Cinque Ports at Hythe, a reception for the Cinque Ports' Association at Walmer Castle, a visit to the Winkle Club at Hastings and a service at St Mary the Virgin, Dover. This was to dedicate a stained glass window as a tribute to members of the RAF air sea rescue unit who had plucked many airmen from the clutches of the sea during the Second World War. As she left the church she complimented the pupils of St Mary's School on their singing of the hymns. Whilst in Dover she sent Ray Warner, well-known Dover photographer and producer of Dover's annual films, a message thanking him for the loan of his 1979 Dover film, which included a film record of Her Majesty's installation as Lord Warden. As *Britannia* sailed away the Queen Mother waved goodbye to the mayor and other guests who had dined on board.

The Lord Warden presides over the Grand Court of Shepway, 1979

The Jetfoil at speed, 1985

## More berths and a jetfoil service

Another two super berths opened in 1980, which were not only double decker but double width, reducing turn round time to one hour. At the Western Docks a fast jetfoil service to Ostend started in 1981, taking 100 minutes for the journey at 60 miles an hour. Back at East, number 4 berth was refurbished in 1983 to allow faster loading and larger vessels.

A presentation to the Queen Mother during her 1982 visit

## Not according to plan

Mishaps and the need to change plans at the last moment dogged the Queen Mother's next visit during June 1982. The helicopter carrying her had to make an emergency landing soon after take off from Windsor, forcing Her Majesty to transfer to a light plane which landed at Manston. She then visited Canterbury and Faversham as planned, returning by helicopter to Dover where she landed at the hoverport to the sound of the customary 21 gun salute from the castle. The short drive to *Britannia*, berthed at the Prince of Wales Pier, was accompanied by cheering crowds enjoying the radiant smile and wave of the Lord Warden. The crew lined the deck of the royal yacht and as she went on board her Royal Standard was raised at the ship's mainmast and her massive Lord Warden's flag was unfurled at the mizzen mast. All this was a change to the original plan of *Britannia* spending the first night of the visit at Ramsgate. The next day was spent visiting Lydd, Rye and Tenterden, but fog prevented use of her helicopter and a car was used instead. The final day did go according to plan with a visit to Folkestone in the morning and Dover Castle in the afternoon to meet representatives of the Cinque Ports' Confederation. Whilst there, she also opened the Maritime England exhibition and met her Deputy Constable of the Castle, Brigadier Richard Hume, at his residence, Constable's Tower.

A very busy Eastern Docks, 1983

## New terminal

A £9 milllion new terminal, including a large airport style departure lounge, opened in 1984 at Eastern Docks to speed foot and coach passengers to and from the ferries. Immigration and Customs clearance outwards was on the first floor level with inward processing on the ground floor. The multi-storey staff car park was also extended. 1985 saw the completion of another reclamation project involving filling in half the Camber and the loss of the original number 1 berth. This provided much needed additional parking for export freight vehicles. A new passenger services building, close to the berths, was also constructed, providing fast food and a supermarket. Number 3 berth was being refurbished to take larger ferries.

## Tragedies

In 1985 Townsend Thoresen (European Ferries) took over Normandy Ferries. By then Dover Harbour Board's work force had topped 1,000. Tragedy struck twice when *The Princess Margaret* hovercraft crashed into the Southern Breakwater with the loss of four lives and again in 1987 when Townsend Thoresen's *Herald of Free Enterprise* capsized off Zeebrugge with the loss of 193 passengers and crew as it sailed for Dover.

*Herald of Free Enterprise*

## New train ferry berth

Despite the Channel Tunnel project, a new train ferry berth was built on Admiralty Pier and completed in 1988. It was designed to accommodate a new ferry, *Nord Pas de Calais*, at any state of the tide. The ferry could carry freight lorries on its upper deck and railway wagons on the lower. The old train ferry dock, opened in 1936, could take up to two and a half hours to pump the water level up to the required height.

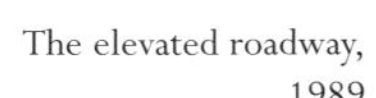

The elevated roadway, 1989

Import freight area packed with lorries, 1988

## More development at the Eastern Docks

At Eastern Docks the new number 1 berth was finished in 1988. It could be used both by deep sea vessels and as a stand-by for ferry berths. In 1988 the reclamation of the rest of the Camber was also completed. This had included the demolition of the two original ro-ro (roll on, roll off) berths, numbers 2 and 3. Their replacements were finished in 1989 ready for new ferries able to carry 2,500 passengers and 600 cars. At the same time another major project was completed in order to separate completely inward from outward traffic. This was achieved by building an elevated four lane roadway 650 metres long, from the berths' assembly area to Immigration and Customs controls.

The Queen Mother and Revd. Alan Simper, 1989

## Celebrating 10 years as Lord Warden

To mark her first ten years as Lord Warden, the Queen Mother visited Dover again in 1989, arriving at noon on *Britannia* on Sunday 4 June as crowds cheered the nation's favourite great grandmother. A royal salute was fired from the castle by 100 (Yeomanry) Regiment of the Royal Artillery Volunteers. Once again it was raining, but this did not dampen the welcome by the Dover lifeboat, harbour tugs and ships dressed over all sounding their sirens. Soon after her arrival, the Queen Mother welcomed on board guests from the Cinque Ports for lunch. Following a reception on board in the early evening, the yacht's Royal Marines band 'beat the retreat' on the pier. The day was not yet over for this lady in her 90th year. After her guests left, she held a private dinner party on board. On Monday morning she attended a special thanksgiving service for her ten years at St Mary's Parish Church and then visited St Mary's Primary School, celebrating its 200th anniversary. Outside the Town Hall she inspected the 100 man guard of honour from the Royal Engineers whilst the national anthem was played by the band of the Royal Green Jackets. Inside the ancient building the Queen Mother as Lord Warden presided at a meeting of the Cinque Ports' Court of Brotherhood and Guestling. Afterwards, she received a great many posies during her walkabout amongst the crowd of well wishers outside. Later, she rejoined *Britannia* at the Prince of Wales Pier and was escorted out of the harbour by *HMS Andromeda*. It was still only 1pm!

The Princess of Wales inspects Customs controls at Dover, 1989

## Diana, Princess of Wales

At the press of a button, Diana, Princess of Wales, destroyed drugs worth £11million when she visited Customs and Excise at Dover on 15 September 1989. This was at the Queen's Warehouse, where Customs and Excise store seized goods imported illegally such as drugs, alcohol and tobacco as well as any transport used in such operations – cars, lorries and coaches. The Princess was then driven to the Eastern Docks in her beige Rolls Royce to see how Customs control the enormous numbers of passengers, cars and freight lorries that use the port. An active campaigner in the fight against illegal drugs, she was given a demonstration of a vehicle search and shown some of the specially designed concealments used by smugglers. From the Terminal Control Tower Jonathan Sloggett, the Managing Director of the Harbour Board, explained how the port managed to process so much traffic in such a confined area of reclaimed land before she was entertained to lunch by the Collector of Customs and Excise, Roy Crossley, and his senior managers at their headquarters, Burlington House. The owner of the building had taken the trouble to redecorate the appropriate ladies' toilet, which in the event the Princess did not use, much to the amusement of the staff. The Princess ended her visit by taking a Channel trip in the Customs cutter *Vigilant*, used to track and intercept suspect vessels. Nobody who met this charming and beautiful lady could have foreseen what the future had in store for her – separation from her husband, Prince Charles, divorce and her tragic death in Paris in 1997.

Eastern Docks at night, 1991

## Privatisation threat

Privatisation of the port was a real threat in 1991, causing concern to the 10,000 people employed directly or indirectly. Calais Chamber of Commerce expressed interest in buying, but the threat eventually receded when the government changed its mind. Despite this uncertainty and the possibility of the Channel Tunnel reducing traffic by half, another new berth, number 7, handling four lanes of traffic simultaneously, was started at Eastern Docks.

The Western Docks in 1987, prior to redevelopment

Wellington Dock transformed into a yacht marina

## Redevelopment of the Western Docks

By 1992 the long-threatened Channel Tunnel was nearing completion and as part of its plans for diversification, the Harbour Board announced a £100 million redevelopment plan for the Western Docks to include a 400 berth yacht marina, an hotel, offices, shops and a restaurant. Use of the inner docks by traditional cargo ships had virtually ceased anyway with increasing use of the Eastern Arm by larger vessels. Provision of temperature controlled fruit storage facilities operated by the George Hammond Group and new berths on the filled-in Camber helped make Dover the UK's third busiest fruit importing centre. During this same busy year the Harbour Board bought the empty Old Park Barracks, covering 225 acres at Whitfield, for redevelopment for port related activities. Port Zone, as it was named, opened in 2000.

Unloading fruit into the new temperature-controlled sheds

## Asylum seekers and terrorists

By 1994 increasing numbers of asylum seekers and economic migrants were arriving at Dover, including many hidden in lorries. This was a major problem for the port for the rest of the decade and beyond. The government introduced fines for lorry drivers carrying migrants, the ferry operators were obliged to carry out checks prior to loading in France and immigration controls at Dover were strengthened considerably, including the use of sniffer dogs. There were several instances of such migrants meeting their deaths in their attempts to evade detection, culminating in the discovery by Customs staff of 58 Chinese dead from suffocation in a lorry.

Terrorist threats also meant a substantial increase in security measures at all ports and airports. Dover was no exception.

## Channel Tunnel opens

The Channel Tunnel finally opened in 1994 albeit with teething problems. Traffic growth was slow. There was an immediate reduction in Dover's ferry business but the impact was not as great as had been expected. A loss of 5,000 jobs had been predicted. However, there were casualties – the Dover-Boulogne and Dover-Ostend ferry services were axed with consequent job losses and Hoverspeed also laid off staff. At the end of 1995 the train ferry service begun in 1936 ended. Western Docks Station, formerly Dover Marine, closed, but was restored and converted into an attractive terminal for the new cruise liner traffic. It opened in 1996 and by 1998 could boast 140 liner calls, necessitating the construction of a second cruise liner terminal on Admiralty Pier. This was completed in 2000. The sight of three and sometimes four cruise liners in port together was impressive as were visits by the 90,000 ton liner *Constellation* from 2002 and the even bigger, 109,000 ton, 290 metres long *Grand Princess* in 2004.

Cruise liners at the Admiralty Pier dwarfing Southern House

*City of London II*

## New lifeboat

Yet another new lifeboat arrived in Dover Harbour in 1997 escorted by the Walmer lifeboat and with a DHB tug firing its water cannon in salute. This was the *City of London II*, costing £1,450,000 and paid for by the RNLI City of London branch. The Duke of Kent had been President of the RNLI since the death of his mother, the previous president, in 1969. He came to name the boat and to pay tribute to the Dover lifeboat crew who operated in some of the world's busiest and most treacherous waters. Since 1855 the Dover lifeboat had saved 859 lives. The coxswain, Tony Hawkins, presented the Duke with an RNLI jumper during his trip round the harbour in the new Severn class boat, which could do 25 knots. Betteshanger Band entertained the guests during a buffet lunch provided in a huge cargo storage shed, now demolished, which had been swept clean and decorated by the crew and supporters of the lifeboat.

## De Bradelei Wharf

The De Bradelei Wharf factory shopping complex opened in 1997 in the converted workshops on Cambridge Road fronting Wellington Dock. It was an immediate success and soon had to be extended with the loss of the old Patent Slipway. During the same year another seven acres were reclaimed at Eastern Docks to accommodate the growing number of unaccompanied freight trailers.

De Bradelei Wharf, Wellington Dock

The Eastern Docks in 1993

## All change

In 1998 P&O Ferries and Stena Line – Stena had taken over from Sea Containers the old British Rail ferry business – merged; although this arrangement only lasted until 2002 when P&O bought out Stena's interests and renamed the company P&O Ferries. With the relocation of Customs clearance facilities for lorries from the Eastern to Western Docks, the Harbour Board purchased Southern House in 1998 to house Customs clearance agents. This was the former Lord Warden Hotel built by the railway company in the mid-nineteenth century for cross-Channel travellers and frequented for 75 years by the royal, the rich and the famous.

Lord Warden Hotel and
Pilot House in the 1850s

## End of duty frees

Day tripper passenger traffic was badly hit in 1999 when duty free concessions for travellers between Member States of the European Community were finally abolished as a consequence of the European Single Market, despite being able to bring in legally since 1993 virtually unlimited quantities of cheap tobacco and alcohol from the continent, provided it was for personal use; Customs staff were kept busy countering large-scale abuse.

## Watersports

There was strong opposition in the town to Harbour Board plans in 1999 for a three-storey watersports centre on the beach in the middle of the sea front and planning permission was eventually refused. However, a less controversial site near the Clock Tower was under discussion in 2004.

The Duke of Edinburgh chats to mariners at the Yacht Club in 2000

The little ships in Dover before leaving for Dunkirk in 2000

# Dunkirk's little ships

The Duke of Edinburgh visited the harbour on 8 June 2000 to see the little ships of Dunkirk make their last official trip to Dunkirk, marking the historic evacuation in 1940. They were all assembled in the Granville Dock. The Duke, who was a naval officer during the Second World War, was greeted on arrival by Raymond Baxter, the broadcaster who was the Honorary Admiral of the Association of Dunkirk Little Ships. The Duke went on board MTB102, a motor torpedo boat, and met its former captain, 83 year old Christopher Dreyer, who had taken part in the operation. This vessel had been the Admiral's flagship during the evacuation and in 1944 had also carried Winston Churchill and General Eisenhower to inspect the D-Day invasion fleet. After meeting many of the seafarers, the Duke boarded the DHB launch, *Director*, to sail round the Granville Dock to get a good look at all the craft whilst wartime songs, like Vera Lynn singing *We'll Meet Again*, were played from one of the boats. Bad weather delayed the departure of this little fleet until the next day and prevented 29 vessels from making the crossing, but eventually 58 ships took part ranging from 26 footers to 104 footers. The Dover lifeboat accompanied them. Some 400 Dunkirk veterans made the crossing by ferry and cast poppies into the

The Duke inspects the fleet of little ships

The first vessels leave harbour for Dunkirk

sea as the *Last Post* was sounded. On the following Sunday a Lancaster bomber dropped 50,000 poppies over the Dunkirk beaches in memory of those who never made it home. During this final official visit by the ageing members of the Dunkirk Veterans Association, 800 of them marched past the Prince of Wales. Sadly, one man aged 82 collapsed and died just before the march.

Following his visit to the little ships, the Duke of Edinburgh visited the Royal Cinque Ports Yacht Club on the sea front. The club was founded in 1862 and is one of the oldest in the country. The Duke of Connaught, a son of Queen Victoria, who had been stationed in Dover as an army officer, was Commodore for its first 60 years. It was he who gave the club the right to fly the Blue Ensign flag. The Duke of Edinburgh, patron of the club for 40 years, met the Commodore and members who presented him with a club tie. Young people from Dover's watersports centre also met him. Before leaving Dover, the Duke went to the castle where the Deputy Constable, Brigadier Trevor Minter, showed him a model of the proposed £40,000 statue of Admiral Sir Bertram Ramsay, who had played such an important part in masterminding the Dunkirk evacuation and the Normandy landings during the Second World War. Unfortunately, he died in an air crash near Paris in 1945. The Duke returned to Dover in 2000 to unveil the statue, which looks out from the Castle Cliff across the Channel to France.

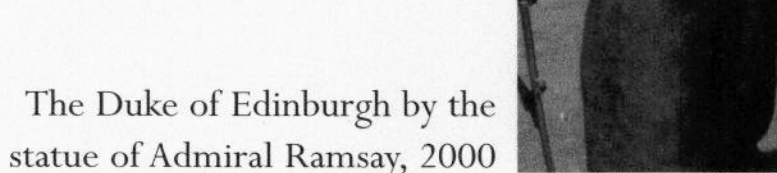

The Duke of Edinburgh by the statue of Admiral Ramsay, 2000

## Happy 100th Birthday

The Queen Mother was in Dover in July 2000, a few days before her 100th birthday on 4 August. On this occasion she did not arrive by sea or even visit the harbour, but flew in by helicopter to the Duke of York's Royal Military School at Guston where the school band played *Happy Birthday* whilst she was welcomed by the Lord Lieutenant of Kent, Lord Kingsdown, and other dignitaries. The Queen Mother was then cheered all the way to the Town Hall where a giant birthday card was presented to her, containing the signatures of hundreds of local people. The cover had been painted by 6 year old Ben Steele of Charlton School. The 14 mayors of the Cinque Ports Confederation were gathered on the steps of the Town Hall to greet the ever-smiling Lord Warden, despite walking with two sticks. They presented her with a watercolour painting of Dover by a local artist, Karl Pitwon, and a scroll of loyal greetings and birthday wishes. Tea with schoolchildren from all the Cinque Ports was followed by a slow drive through the town centre with the bells of St Mary's Church competing with the cheers of the crowd. The next day the Lord Warden held a reception in the grounds of Walmer Castle, her official residence, for representatives of the Cinque Ports Confederation. As always, she attended church on Sunday morning. On this occasion she went to St Mary in the Castle and then had lunch with her Deputy Constable at his residence, Constable's Tower. This grand old lady died in 2001.

Hovercraft leaving port in 1982

## Hovercraft out, Seacats in

October 2000 saw the last hovercraft flights from Dover after 32 years. Hoverspeed replaced the two hovercraft with catamarans called Seacats, operating from the Hoverport.

## The end of the century

By the end of the century the Port of Dover and the Channel Tunnel had almost equal shares of the greatly increased cross-Channel traffic. During 2000 7,000 people were employed in the port on ship or shore, handling 16.2 million passengers (compared with 21 million in 1977), 2.6 million cars, over 148,000 coaches and 1.6 million lorries.

The inner harbour transformed into a marina

The Bronze Age Boat, preserved and on display at Dover Museum

Prince Charles at the Bronze Age Boat Gallery in 2000

## Bronze Age Boat

Charles, Prince of Wales, visited Dover in March 2000 to view the preserved Bronze Age Boat in its special gallery in Dover Museum. This boat, possibly used for cross-Channel trade, dates from 1550BC and was excavated in Dover in 1992. Prince Charles did not visit the port on this occasion, but on 20 May 2003 he made a private visit to Customs and Excise at the Eastern Docks after arriving by helicopter. This visit was the result of a conversation when investing a Customs officer with an MBE (Member of the Order of the British Empire) at Buckingham Palace. The Prince expressed an interest in seeing the work of the officer. He was shown how Customs make use of intelligence and technology to intercept those passengers, cars and freight vehicles most likely to be evading duty and tax on large quantities of alcohol and tobacco or attempting to import illegally prohibited drugs, whilst still allowing the vast majority of port users to move quickly through the busy port. He was amongst the first to visit the recently-updated Customs car examination facilities equipped to strip down vehicles.

## Faster movement and more berths

A 26-lane check-in 'plaza' opened at the Eastern Docks in 2002 for outward bound vehicles. This speeded up processing prior to loading on to the ferries from an average of 21 minutes per car to 11 minutes and from 28 to 14 minutes for freight vehicles. For vehicles arriving by ferry average times from arrival to dock exit in 2003 were 14 minutes for cars and 12 minutes for lorries.

To cope with expected traffic increases and a new generation of longer and wider ferries a new jetty was completed in 2004 at the Eastern Docks, providing new berths 8 and 9 complemented by an extension to the elevated roadway to service them.

New passenger facilities

## Royal visit

Throughout 2005, the 200th anniversary of the Battle of Trafalgar, Dover with the rest of the nation is celebrating its maritime heritage under the Sea Britain 2005 banner. It is, therefore, most fitting that Her Majesty Queen Elizabeth II has decided to revisit this famous port of kings and queens on 20 July 2005.

# Chapter 5 Today and tomorrow

*Today's Port of Dover – one of the world's busiest and most successful ports*

Dover is one of the UK's trust ports, which means that it is an independent statutory body governed by its own unique act of parliament and controlled by an independent board. All its profits –£4.6 million after tax in 2004 – are re-invested in the port to maintain and improve services. The Harbour Board now has eight members. The Secretary of State for Transport appoints the non-executive chairman and four of the non-executive members. The fifth non-executive member and the two executive members, including the managing director, are appointed by the Board itself. Appointments are no longer for life!

Today's Port of Dover is one of the world's busiest and most successful ports. Dover is also the UK's second busiest cruise liner port and the third busiest UK port handling perishable goods – over 263,000 tonnes in 117 vessels in 2004. It also boasts a 400 berth marina facility. In 2004 the port handled 1.95 million freight vehicles, 2.5 million tourist cars and 128,000 coaches. 126 cruise ships called during the year, carrying 178,000 passengers.

The Harbour Board's estate includes commercial offices, retail and leisure outlets, residential apartments, car parks and facilities for statutory bodies such as Customs and Immigration.

The high cost of reclaiming land from the sea – £2.5 million per hectare – means that the use of this existing scarce resource has to be optimised, resulting in frequent changes to the infrastructure and facilities.

The Harbour Board, in its constant search for improvements which are so important in order to maintain and increase the prosperity of the port and the local economy, is pressing the highway authority for a new ground level exit from the Eastern Docks. Similarly, with other partners it is lobbying for a fast rail passenger service to London, the dualling of the A2 highway from Lydden to Eastern Docks to alleviate the Townwall Street congestion and pollution as well as promoting a reduction in road freight by increased use of rail.

As a major company in the Dover area, the Harbour Board also contributes to strategic long-term planning as well as involving itself in the current life of the town.

What does the future hold? Our story ends with the Harbour Board working on a 30-year master plan to cope with the expected future growth in traffic and opportunities to handle it within the limits of the present harbour. Difficult questions have to be addressed, such as will the Eastern Docks run out of capacity and, if so, when? Will additional capacity at the Western Docks be needed?

With a long and historic past, Dover's harbour still has an important role to play in the life of the nation, even though with the advent of air travel royal visitors are much rarer these days. During its 400 year history the Harbour Board may not always have carried out its responsibilities effectively, but, as it enters its fifth century, it is certainly a 'going concern' eager to meet whatever challenges the future may hold.

Meanwhile, it carries out its day to day responsibilities: maintaining several miles of piers and roads, sheds and offices, berths, cranes, lighthouses, navigational aids, conducting hydrographic surveys, keeping the harbour dredged, maintaining the sea defences, providing essential services to the dock area and policing it. It also takes pride in keeping the promenade and beach attractive both for Dovorians and visitors. Long may it continue!

# Appendix 1 Kings and Queens of England

| | |
|---|---|
| 1066 | William I |
| 1087 | William II |
| 1100 | Henry I |
| 1135 | Stephen |
| 1154 | Henry II |
| 1189 | Richard I |
| 1199 | John |
| 1216 | Henry III |
| 1272 | Edward I |
| 1307 | Edward II |
| 1327 | Edward III |
| 1377 | Richard II |
| 1399 | Henry IV |
| 1413 | Henry V |
| 1422 | Henry VI |
| 1461 | Edward IV |
| 1483 | Edward V |
| 1483 | Richard III |
| 1485 | Henry VII |
| 1509 | Henry VIII |
| 1547 | Edward VI |
| 1553 | Mary I |
| 1558 | Elizabeth I |
| 1603 | James I |
| 1625 | Charles I |
| 1649 | The Commonwealth |
| 1660 | Charles II |
| 1685 | James II |
| 1689 | William III and Mary II |
| 1702 | Anne |
| 1714 | George I |
| 1727 | George II |
| 1760 | George III |
| 1820 | George IV |
| 1830 | William IV |
| 1837 | Victoria |
| 1901 | Edward VII |
| 1910 | George V |
| 1936 | Edward VIII |
| 1936 | George VI |
| 1952 | Elizabeth II |

# Appendix 2 Chairmen of Dover Harbour Board formerly Wardens and Assistants of Dover Harbour

1606 Earl of Northampton
1614 Earl of Somerset
1615 Lord Zouch of Haryngworth
1624 Duke of Buckingham
1628 Earl of Suffolk
1640 Duke of Lennox and Richmond
1642 Sir Edward Boys
1646 Major John Boys
1648 Sir Algernon Sydney
1651 Lt. Colonel Thomas Kelsey
1656 Colonel John Lambert and Admiral Robert Blake
1660 Earl of Winchelsea
1660 Prince James, Duke of York
1669 Earl of Winchelsea
1689 Colonel John Beaumont
1691 Earl of Romney
1702 George, Prince of Denmark
1708 Duke of Dorset
1713 Duke of Ormonde
1714 Duke of Dorset
1717 Earl of Leicester
1728 Duke of Dorset
1765 Earl of Holdernesse
1778 Earl of Guilford
1792 Rt. Hon. William Pitt
1806 Earl of Liverpool
1829 Duke of Wellington
1853 Marquess of Dalhousie
1861 Viscount Palmerston
1866 Earl Granville
1891 Rt. Hon. W. H. Smith
1891 Marquess of Dufferin and Ava
1895 Marquess of Salisbury
1904 Lord Curzon of Kedleston
1906 Sir William Crundall
1934 Vice Admiral Sir H. Percy Douglas
1940 Admiral Sir Aubrey Smith
1950 Henry T. Hawksfield
1965 Vice Admiral Sir Archibald Day
1970 Admiral of the Fleet Sir Michael le Fanu
1971 Sir Clifford Jarrett
1980 Sir William Harris
1983 Sir Frederic Bolton
1989 John Maltby
1996 Adam Broadbent
2001 Robert Dibble

# Bibliography

*Royal Visitors by John H Mowll 1937*

*Dover & the Monarchy 1066-1688 Ivan Green Triangle Publications 2001*

*Dover at War by Roy Humphreys published by Alan Stroud Publishing Ltd, Stroud 1993.*

*History Today Companion to British History, Juliet Gardiner and Neil Wenborn, Collins and Brown Ltd 1995*

*Stories of Dover and the Grand Tour by C.L.W. Smith, published privately 1981*

*Our town, Dover 1945-2000 by Derek Leach and Terry Sutton, published by Riverdale Publications 2003*

*Annals of Dover by J Bavington Jones*

*The Story of the Dover Lifeboats by Jeff Morris 1998*

*Various issues of The Dover Society Newsletter*

*The History of Dover Harbour by Alec Hasenson published by Aurum Special Editions 1980*

*Portcullis – house journal of HM Customs & Excise*

*Gateway of England by Rivers Scott, Dover Harbour Board 1956.*

*History of the Castle, Town and Port of Dover by Revd. S. P. H. Statham*
*published by Longmans Green & Co London 1899*

*History of Dover and Dover Castle by W. Batcheller, published by Batcheller Libraries of Dover c1830*

*When Was That? by J. Bavington Jones published by Dover Express.*

*The Normans – History of a Dynasty by David Crouch published by Hambledon and London 2002*

*Edward I by Michael Prestwich published by Guild Publishing London 1988*

*Life and Times of Richard I by John Gillingham published by Weidenfeld and Nicolson 1973*

*Debrett's Kings and Queens of Britain by David Williamson published by Webb and Bower 1986*

# Acknowledgements

For their help in researching illustrations I must thank the staff of Dover Museum and Dover Library. I am also very grateful to the following organisations and individuals for allowing me to use their images: the Imperial War Museum, the British Museum, the Kent Messenger Group, the Dover Express, Bob Hollingsbee, Joe Harman, Anthony Lane and, of course, Dover Harbour Board.

## Image Libraries used

Mary Evans Picture Library
Popperfoto
The Bridgeman Art Library
The National Archives
Getty Images
Empics